# Let's talk abou

# Child to Parent Violence or Aggression

**Dr Wendy Thorley and Mr Al Coates MBE**

CEL&T

**About the Authors**

## Dr Wendy Thorley PhD, M.Ed, B.A (Hons) Ed. R.G.N. National Teaching Fellow HEA

Is an experienced lecturer and practitioner with more than 20 years' experience of teaching and training. Whilst at the University of Sunderland she was involved in several programmes as a consultant and programme leader, including: BA (Hons) Childhood Studies, BA (Hons) Applied Family Studies, Early Years Professional Status, Foundation Degree in Education and Care, BA (Hons) Education and Care, Higher Level Teaching Assistant and Masters Teaching and Learning as well as developing several CPD modules from Level 4-7 in Mental Health and Dyslexia. She has extensive experience of collaborative partnerships with further education colleges and Local Authority organisations for continuing professional development (CPD). Within her role of Senior lecturer at University of Sunderland she led her department in developing the use of technological innovations to enhance the learning experience. Starting her career in the NHS, she undertook a range of CPD initiatives to develop her teaching and learning expertise. She gained professional experience initially in Nurse Education prior to returning to HE for Primary Education study. She has held positions in Local Authority Social Services Human Resource Department (HRD) related programmes before consolidating her experience first in Further Education then moving into Higher Education. She is highly regarded across voluntary and statutory organisations locally and regionally and has published a range of papers, completed national and regional consultancy roles and invited key note speaker contributions. In addition to her professional qualifications she has completed: The Child Trauma Academy- NMT Advanced Clinical Practice Training Series and NMT interventions for supporting traumatised children, the Further Education and Adult Teaching Certificate and Internal Verifiers Award as well as Vocational and Skills Trainer and Assessor, Human Resource Development (Level 4), HE Diploma: Further Education and Training, the Youth Trainers Award, and HE Diploma - Primary Education in addition to Counselling in the development of learning. alongside numerous CPD achievements including counselling the bereaved.

## Mr Al Coates MBE BSc Social Work

Is an experienced Social Worker who has extensive knowledge of Fostering, independent Social Work as well as Social Work Practice Educator and Trainer. As a member of the Department for Education's Expert Advisory Group on Adoption Support (now replaced by Adopter Reference Group) he has undertaken to help support families who adopt, recognising these children and young people who are adopted can present with a wide range of challenging behaviours. As a father of 6 Adopted Children he is well aware of the diverse needs of children who are adopted. In addition, managing his own Foster Care caseload and working with those who Foster as well as those who provide residential settings for children who are Looked After, he understands that children and young people can often display behaviour that can be viewed as unacceptable, aggressive or violent; and managing these behaviours places immense pressure on those within the family setting. Mr Coates runs a popular blogging site at alcoates.co.uk; for which he was awarded First4Adoptions blogger of the year in 2015 and 2016. He also produces the Adoption and Fostering Podcast which is available at: http://adoptionandfostering.podbean.com. In recognition to his commitment and work he was awarded his MBE in the New Years Honours list, January 2018. He has presented at a number of events as a Key Note Speaker and an invited contributor at regional and National conferences and events, discussing Child to Parent Violence or Aggression, following the success of the CPV publications with Dr Wendy Thorley in January 2017.

**Related Publications**

- Thorley and Coates (2017a) Child-Parent Violence(CPV): an exploratory exercise available at: . Amazon Publications[https://www.academia.edu/30962152/Child_-Parent_Violence_CPV_an_exploratory_exercise](https://www.academia.edu/30962152/Child_-Parent_Violence_CPV_an_exploratory_exercise)

- Thorley W and Coates A (2017b) Child - Parent Violence (CPV): Impact on parent/carers available at: [http://www.academia.edu/31433287/Child_-Parent_Violence_CPV_exploratory_exercise_Impact_on_parent_carers_when_living_with_CPV](http://www.academia.edu/31433287/Child_-Parent_Violence_CPV_exploratory_exercise_Impact_on_parent_carers_when_living_with_CPV)

- Thorley W and Coates A (2017c) Child - Parent Violence (CPV): Grappling with an Enigma. available at: [http://www.academia.edu/32167527/Child_-Parent_Violence_CPV_Grappling_with_an_Enigma](http://www.academia.edu/32167527/Child_-Parent_Violence_CPV_Grappling_with_an_Enigma)

## Acknowledgements:

We are very grateful to Helen Townsend for the use of her illustrations. Helen provides a substantial number of resources for parents, schools and professionals supporting children who have experienced loss or trauma at: [www.innerworldwork.co.uk](www.innerworldwork.co.uk).

We would also like to thank all of those families who took the time to complete the survey and provide us with this insight into their world. We wish every single family the very best in accessing and gaining the support they need. We fully recognise that at best this is only a snapshot of the day to day living they encounter as families with children who engage in CPVA.

## Copyright:

*Suggested citation:*
Thorley W and Coates A (2018) Let's Talk About: Child to Parent Violence or Aggression. KDP-Amazon Publishers

# Contents

**Glossary of terms**

ACE: Adverse Childhood Experience

CPVA: Child to Parent Violence and Aggression

EHCP: Educational Health Care Plan

SEND: Special Educational Needs and Disability

# Section 1: Let's Talk About:

## Child to Parent Violence or Aggression (CPVA)

*In the varied topography of professional practice, there is a high, hard ground overlooking a swamp. On the high ground manageable problems lend themselves to solution through application of research-based theory and technique. In the swampy lowland, messy, confusing problems defy technical solution.* Schon (1987)

This report sets out the findings of the CPVA 2018 survey completed in January- February 2018. The aim of this survey hoped to reflect what had evolved following the initial exploratory exercise of 2017 (Thorley and Coates 2017a, 2017b and 2017c). The main aim of the previous survey, in 2017, was to open up the issue of CPVA for families. The response to the publications, following the 2017 survey, has been in some ways, beyond that anticipated. The report publications were accessed across 34 countries and over 300 cities, indicating that CPVA is a far wider concern than had been anticipated when the 2016/2017 survey was set out. Further developments have seen a range of conferences and events include CPVA, as part of discussions or input; in addition, there has been funding made available to PAC-UK for example, that enables parents to undertake training in Non-Violent Resistance programmes developed by Coogan (2011, 2014 and 2018) and Coogan and Lister (2015). Since the beginning of 2017, alongside the release of the reports by Thorley and Coates, there has been a general raising of awareness of CPVA that has built on the work of Helen Bonnick (Holes in the Wall), Amanda Boorman (The Open Nest) and publications in academic forums; such as that of Holt (2013, 2016), Coogan (2011, 2014, 2018) and Selwyn et al (2013, 2014). Adoption UK (2018) published a special edition of Adoption Today, focused exclusively on CPVA with a range of contributors and individual family members. Although emerging and existing intervention models have been promoted, to help support those families living with CPVA, there remains a significant number of families still waiting for support; such as those who experience CPVA from birth children rather than adopted children, as well as those parents whose children engage in CPVA as a consequence of the child's Special Educational Needs and Disability (SEND).

The findings of the 2017 reports were purposely made open access, to enable them to reach as wide an audience as possible; including professionals, parents and carers. More importantly, this enabled those who had participated, in the data generated to access the reports based on their experiences. To that purpose the reports were advertised through social media platforms, such as Twitter and Facebook, and subsequently retweeted and shared multiple times. The level of social media sharing further demonstrated the value that parents placed on the reports and that the reports validated their views, alongside providing insight into their lived experience. Linked articles and press releases were distributed through the websites of Adoption UK, Community Care and the Huffington Post; with the findings being generally accepted as accurate and reflective of many family's experiences. Building on this publicity led to a wider range of discussions alongside a demand for moving the discussions further, this involved a range of organisations and individuals. There was a genuine interest in finding out more about CPVA, as well as a desire to understand CPVA, by a range of professionals and parents. Discussions involved children and families, fostering and adoption social workers (based in local authority teams as well as the independent sector), alongside the Community Care Live Conference (September 2017). There was acknowledgement by a significant majority of those, who attended these events, that CPVA was a known occurrence in a range of families; however, it also appeared that none of the professionals spoken to had received specific training, or practice advice, in relation to supporting families living with CPVA. Whilst concerning, the lack of training for professionals supporting families living with CPVA was not unexpected; this reflected the findings from the previous reports (2017) that suggested support offered was inconsistent or ineffective. In addition to information sharing across social media and local events, the findings were presented to the Department of Education Expert Advisory Group on Adoption Support. This group felt strongly that CPVA was an issue that needed attention, particularly at a time when workforce development and practice were also being reviewed; this in turn led to a meeting with Isabelle Trowler, the then Chief Social Worker for children in England. Such discussions helped open up the reality of living with CPVA for all families, particularly those whose children have SEND, enabling Yvonne Newbold[1] to discuss this within radio broadcasts, such as Victoria Derbyshire, and in interviews across a range of media both in press and in broadcast.

Whilst we are not suggesting that all of these developments were directly related to the publication of the 2017 research reports, or any ensuing discussions; what appears to be

---

[1] For more information relating to the work of Yvonne Newbold go to www.yvonnenewbold.com where a range of blogs are available discussing VCB along with information on training available for families

evident is that CPVA is now discussed more publicly and openly, with an increasing awareness of CPVA for those parents whose children have SEND. It therefore seemed appropriate to 'take stock' of what has developed so far, in order to inform any future progress or practice. That parents are talking about living with CPVA is in itself a major development, one that moves CPVA from a 'hidden' issue impacting upon families, to one that is recognised more openly. Whilst there continues to be much to address and much to understand, placing this into public debate is the first step of accepting that not only does CPVA exist, but that CPVA is a very real concern for many families within our society here and now.

The main issue when attempting to generate a more comprehensive dialogue with parents is reflected in the 'nature of the beast', in that very many parents do not, or will not, discuss violence within the home environment; be this adult to adult/ child to adult/ adult to child. This means it is fully recognised that there are limitations to the data collected[2]. However, the issue of CPVA is such, that without these 'voices and opinions', any discussion relating to potential interventions, or generating a more comprehensive dialogue, may miss what it is these families living with CPVA need and when this is needed. For this reason, whilst it is fully acknowledged the validity and reliability of the data reported may be compromised, because of using social media platforms, the findings are representative of the voices of those CPVA impacts upon the most. In this way, whilst academically it may be argued that the robustness of the data does not reflect rigorous research protocols, the data does support exploratory research frameworks.

Exploratory research provides the opportunity to explore existing problems, rather than attempting to offer final and conclusive solutions to existing problems (see for example Bulmer, 1977; Crotty, 1998; Stebbings, 2001; Cohen et al, 2005; Bryman, 2015; Walliman, 2015). The purpose of this survey was to set out to explore, more comprehensively, the issues raised since the 2017 survey and publications (Thorley and Coates 2017a, b and c). In this way, the data generated built on what Alvesson and Skoldberg (2000, p.2) proposed, in so much that *"empirical social science is very much less certain and more problematic than common sense or conventional methodological textbooks would have us think."* They go onto argue and support debate linked to the interwoven aspects of linguistic, social, political and theoretical aspects; that are integrated in the process of emerging comprehension, suggesting it is during

---

[2] The survey was published via Google Forms and promoted via social media such as Twitter and Facebook for anonymous response, given the sensitive nature of the questions. The survey was also promoted by organisations representing a range of family groups that supported their members who experienced CPVA.

this process empirical research is developed. This survey achieved insight into further understanding of a complex issue that by nature includes aspects of linguistic, social, political and theoretical aspects. In this way, this survey commenced as a reflective exercise that enabled this report to 'take stock' in order to move forward, as explained by Alvesson, Skoldberg (ibid., p.5)

> *"Empirical research in a reflective mode starts from a sceptical approach to what appear to be at a superficial glance as unproblematic replicas of the way reality functions, while at the same time maintaining the belief that the study of suitable (well thought out) excerpts from this reality can provide an important basis for a generation of knowledge that opens up rather than closes, and furnishes opportunities for understanding rather than establishes truths"*

The comments made by Alvesson and Skoldberg (ibid.) relate to the ambiguity of empirical research, recognising that interpretations are multifaceted, complex and include the relationship between translation and reader. In addition to the data generated, further complexities arise in translating and correlating the findings, that are outlined in Gadamer's (1979) philosophical hermeneutics; whereby human understanding remains irrevocably biased. This is particularly pertinent to this study given the medium used for generating the parent/ carer voice. In this sense, hermeneutics may offer the grounding for subjectivist research, built upon interpretation and subjectivism, and thereby acknowledges understanding can be found, whilst at the same time cannot be found, within literary terms. However, if discussion of responses generated are not presented, then those parents/ carers who participated remain unheard, on an issue that very much impacts upon not only their families directly but also society generally.

The biggest challenge when discussing CPVA in any forum is trying to define exactly what CPVA is. As argued by Thorley and Coates (2017c) defining CPVA is metaphorically 'Grappling with an Enigma'. They argue that complexity arises when attempting to define what CPVA is specifically, due to the limitation that definitions proposed or outlined can create. Alongside terminology limitations, Coogan (2015) notes that many parents themselves do not identify their child's behaviour as CPVA (a factor also noted by Wilcox and Pooley, 2015); rather parents note difficult relationships or difficult instances, as opposed to contextualising the emerging pattern of behaviour as CPVA. Further ambiguity surrounds the prevalence of CPVA which is vague and obscure, in that this varies from a reported 10% (1:10) to 3%. Stevenson (2016) reported that as many as 1:10 parents experience parent abuse based on research led by Dr Wilcox into *'Responding To Child to Parent Violence';* a Pan European Project that sought to address concerns about increasing reported incidences of CPVA in Spain, Bulgaria, Ireland, Sweden and England. In contrast Bonnick (2016) points to 3% being the figure that most professionals concur (citing Gallagher's discussions); whilst Selwyn and Meakins (2015) point to discrepancies of between 3% and 27%. Whilst there has be little real coverage across general media, there is evidence of CPVA over time; for example, Winterman (2009) reported several cases whilst Cassidy (2012) reported concerns over suggested increasing numbers of CPVA particularly in adoptive family units. One of the difficulties in determining the frequency or incidence of CPVA, both within families and across society, is the lack of focused statistical evidence of CPVA specifically. The main contributing factor for lack of evidenced data, relating to CPVA concerns, stems from the family unit themselves and as with domestic violence, for example, much of these instances remain unreported.

Child on Parent Violence or Aggression was first noted as different to other forms of inter family violence by Harbin and Madden (1979) when they used the term *'Battered Parents'.* They argued that battered parents related to *both to actual physical assault and to verbal and nonverbal threats of physical harm'* (1979 Abstract) and that the majority of the case studies they employed (they examined 43 case studies for their study) involved adolescent males. They also pointed to indicators as well as family subtleties or undercurrents that were notably different to those related to domestic violence or child abuse leading to a proposed definition that suggests CPVA is *'Any harmful act by a child, whether physical, psychological or financial, which is intended to gain power and control over a parent or carer',* which has then be employed in subsequent studies over time; for example by Patterson *et al* (2002), Coogan (2011) Holt (2013) Coogan and Lauster (2015) and Coogan (2018). However, the term itself can be negotiable between Adolescent to Parent Violence and Abuse (APVA), Adolescent to Parent Abuse (APA) and Child on Parent Violence (CPV) to name a few, collectively reflecting Child to Parent Violence and Aggression. Nevertheless, when discussing CPVA as Child to Parent Violence or Aggression, it is worth recognising that 'child' can also represent adolescents, given the legal definition of who a 'child' is, for example in the United Nations Convention on the Rights of the Child, a child as anyone under 18 years of age (Office of the High Commissioner for Human Rights, 1989). This definition of 'child' is also reflected within legislation across England, Wales and Northern Ireland; whereby a child is anyone who has not reached their 18th birthday. In this way discussion about CPVA can include all children and young people under the age of 18, and if adding the Special Educational Needs and Disability

(SEND) indicators, all children and adolescents up to the age of 25 years (as noted within the Children and Family Act, 2014).

Within current discourse there is a repeated acknowledgement that a heightened recognition for CPVA is fundamental to providing support for families living with and experiencing CPVA. However, whilst discussion continues, including that of Labour MP Toby Perkins who raised CPVA within the Houses of Parliament (February 2018), the transfer from theory into practice appears to continue at a slow rate. More importantly such discussion has broadened to include those families whose children have identified Special Educational Needs or Disabilities (SEND) that may display CPVA as a consequence. It is therefore imperative that, when discussing CPVA, all families are recognised and represented in any future planning, policy or legislative change. The need for this to be recognised was highlighted by Adfam and Against Violence and Abuse (2012 p.3) following their project funded by the Department of Health: *"Children's violence and abuse to parents is poorly recognised and caught within a grey area of understanding. As with adult perpetrators, children can be both loving and charming one minute and violent and abusive the next. Satisfactory explanations for this change in behaviour have yet to be found".* Whilst these comments are noted in 2012, the Labour MP Toby Perkins continues to highlight the same issues and concerns in 2018, suggesting and confirming that little has changed in real terms for families living with CPVA.

Part of the issue raised when discussing CPVA is how society recognises children holding a position of 'power' over their family and those adults within their home environment. Following this view, points to CPVA being an issue that society overall struggles to conceptualise, in that adults are perceived to be in control and hold the power position, particularly over their children. This can lead to CPVA being viewed as arguably a misnomer when applying the 'stronger person' lens, in that parents/carers are vulnerable to their children whilst continuing to hold the position of *"socially and economically more power, and in some cases they are stronger physically"* (Ibabe, 2016; p.1538). These arguments then support questions about why parents are unable to 'control' their children. Building on this position then enables any response or support or intervention recommended, to focus on the parent/ carer rather than the child by perceiving the root cause of CPVA to be 'the parents fault'. Such misnomer leads to many parents do seek help to be provided with 'positive parenting classes' and in this way confirms a notion of 'blaming the parent' as a parent problem that requires 'fixing'. Such viewpoints fail to recognise the complexities of family dynamics and the variable family typologies across society, that may increase the prevalence and incidence of CPVA occurring. There are many reasons why CPVA is not reported by families including parents feeling ashamed, humiliated, self-conscious or confused by their child's behaviour (Kennair and Mellor, 2007; Kuay et al, 2017). For some families reporting can become age dependant, in that parent/ carers may be concerned about how the child will react and respond following their reporting of the CPVA, particularly if reporting their concerns will escalate CPVA. Alternatively, the behaviour may be viewed as age-stage normative and the issue is not so much CPVA but an overly anxious parent (Gallagher, 2014).

Where CPVA occurs, for the majority of parents/ carers, only those within the immediate family (who live in the same household) are aware of the behaviour occurring; this in part may be due to 'ownership' of the issue, in that parent/ carers may feel ultimately responsible for their child's behaviour. Such views are supported by legal and social perceptions that encompass notions of 'blame the parent' and address the 'poor parenting' of children, who behave in ways that could be construed as socially unacceptable (as previously noted by Margolin and Baucom, 2014). However, despite the lack of real information to ascertain the level of CPVA overall across the UK, Condry and Miles (2014) noted that there were 1892 cases of CPVA reported to Children's Services in London, over a two-year period, and the majority of children engaging in CPVA for these reported cases were aged 13-19 years old.

This report presents the findings generated from the 2018 CPVA survey, reflecting the opinions of 538 respondents, collected over a four-week period (from release of the survey). With recognition of the limitation social media platforms can have, for survey responses, using social media platforms enabled a wide range of participants to engage, irrespective of where in the UK they lived. More importantly using social media platforms enabled sharing of the survey via dedicated network groups such as that managed by Yvonne Newbold for parents with children who have SEND. The majority (90%) of responses were generated from England and represented voices from across all regions of England as follows:

- South East 19%
- South West 12.5%
- North East 8%
- East Midlands 5%
- Greater London 8%
- East of England 5.5%

- Yorkshire and Humber 7%
- West Midlands 9%
- North West 16%.

For this reason, it cannot be presumed that CPVA is predominantly evident in one regional area to another, therefore any future discussion should reflect a national approach rather than a regionalised approach. Adopting a national collaborative approach recognises that CPVA is not solely an issue impacting upon families in England, subsequently any approach, intervention or strategy needs to benefit families across all of Great Britain. Within the responses received from parent/ carers 4% lived in Wales[3]; 5% lived in Scotland[4] and 1% lived in Northern Ireland[5]; highlighting the need to adopt a collaborative Great Britain response. A further 0.5% resided outside of the UK, this resonates with previous indicators that CPVA is not only across all of society but also across 'Borders and Countries'.

An interesting aspect emerged within the general information relating to the age of the parent/carer experiencing CPVA. As the 21st century progresses so does the age of first time mothers, popular media has noted this trend for more than a decade, one in which first time pregnancies are increasingly seen in woman between 30-40 years of age. This trend reflected the findings of the 2018 survey whereby the majority of parent/ carers participating in the survey were aged 46-55 years old (46%) or aged 36-45 (39%) (as shown in chart 1).

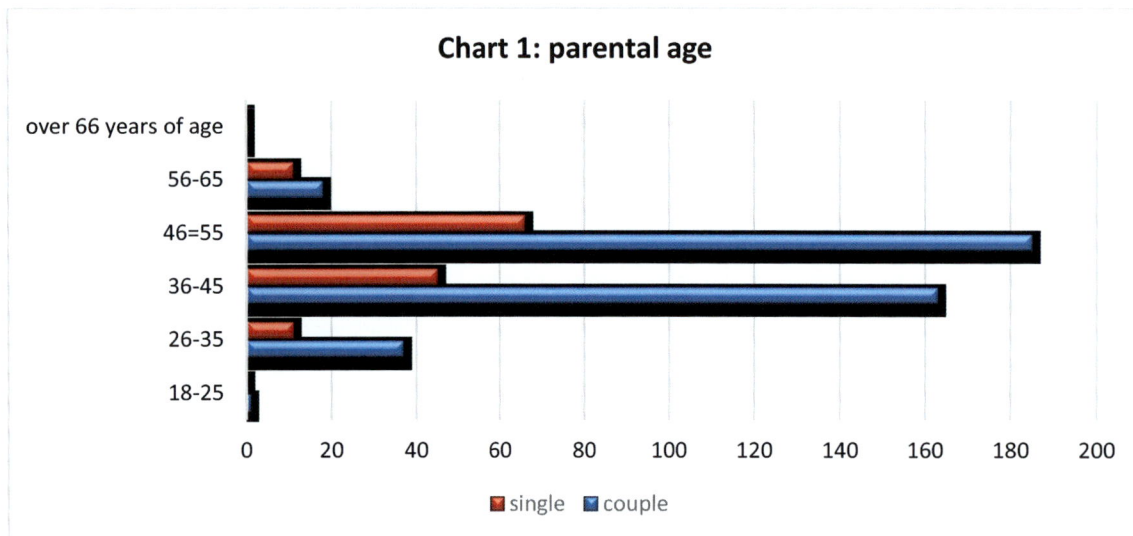

Chart 1: parental age

---

[3] Participants resided in South West Wales, South East Wales, Mid Wales, North West Wales and North East Wales reflective of all Regional areas in Wales
[4] Participants resided in Glasgow, Central Scotland, North East Scotland, the Borders, Lothian and Edinburgh, Mid Scotland and Fife, Strathclyde, Dumfries and Galloway reflective of all but one region across Scotland
[5] These participants resided in Tyrone and Antrim

If such responses are reflected against the findings within Thorley and Coates (2017a), that points to the majority of children displaying CPVA to be aged 6 years, this would suggest these families became parents as older parents. The concern raised from such indicators is the capacity of the parent/ carer to 'restrain' their child should this be advisable in order to protect their child from harm. As the child ages so do the parents, it is therefore not unreasonable to propose parent/ carers aged 55 years or more may seriously struggle to contain their teenager (adolescent's) child's behaviour no matter how many 'parenting' courses they attend. It is for this reason CPVA needs to be not only recognised but addressed as early as possible in order to prevent or reduce the risk of the behaviour becoming 'entrenched' or escalating as the child develops and matures; such concerns may be of particular relevance for single parent/carers who may not have the support of another adult. As detailed within Chart 1 there was only one respondent aged 18-25 years whilst 9% of parent/carers were aged 26-35 and 5% aged 56-65 years old. Responses received represented parent/carers residing as a couple as well as those who were a single parent/carer across all age ranges.

To explore the issues for these parent/ carers, when living with CPVA, this report considers the following areas in more detail:

**Section 2: Let's Talk About: Families Living with CPVA:**

Section 2 considers family typologies in order to consider if there is a heightened risk, of CPVA occurring, within specific types of families. The discussion reflects on how family 'types' are identified, including how these build perceptions of those who seek support for CPVA. In this way, this section question's how family 'types' are categorised and how such labels may, in themselves, create misnomers or barriers for families living with CPVA. Within this section consideration is given to siblings living within the family home, who do not engage in CPVA but are witness to CPVA. Such information raises real concerns for the wellbeing of these siblings.  This section highlights how and why focusing on family types alone does not provide sufficient information regarding increased risk of CPVA occurrence.  Within this section argument for viewing CPVA as a form of domestic violence is asserted, particularly where more than one child resides within the family home. This chapter points to areas of CPVA impact that are currently overlooked, the first of which considers children with SEND particularly birth children. The second area is that of 'harm' to siblings exposed to CPVA whilst living with violence in home environment. This chapter highlights the necessity of Adverse Childhood Experiences to be recognised within any study of children who engage in CPVA behaviours as an influencing factor, and argues such recognition needs to include both pre and post- natal factors that may impact upon the child directly.

**Section 3:  Let's Talk About: Age-Stage Expectations and Behaviour**

Section 3 interrogates behaviours displayed by those children engaging in CPVA, and how these differ from any proposed age-stage developmental norms. In doing so, this section raises questions around society expectation of behaviour as key stage developmental norms, that can prejudice responses to those families living with CPVA should they seek support. Options for support are explored and raise questions around what is available for families at this current time, alongside the barriers of accessing these routes of support. This section highlights the complex multi-faceted nature of CPVA behaviours recognising the real risk these children who engage in CPVA pose, not only to the parent/ carer but also to siblings within the home. In this way consideration is paid to siblings, who may not engage in CPVA but may be subjected to violence and aggression as 'sibling abuse'; an area that is little explored within discussion around CPVA to date. This section argues for a redrafting of the Child Safety Order that exists within the Crime and Disorder Act (1998). Whilst it is recognised that this Order places the child under the supervision of the Youth Offending Team, in England and Wales, the potential for rethinking its application is notable. The Child Safety Order is designed to provide multi-agency supportive interventions, as a proactive approach to reducing the risk of children under the age of 10 behaving in such a way that once they are over the age of 10 (the age of criminality within England and Wales) could result in criminal prosecution. Due to the existence of Home Office Guidance (2015), for Adolescent to Parent Violence, those children under the age of 10 years are overlooked. This means that these children, engaging in CPVA, tend to also be overlooked for support and do not receive sufficient timely intervention. Whilst the Child Support Order would not leave a 'criminal' footprint on the child's details, for when they are older and seeking employment; however, charges made after 10 years of age might leave a 'criminal' footprint and limit life opportunities for these children. The restriction in using the Child Safety Order is based upon the wording used for application of the Order, in that, this cannot be used if the behaviour is within the home environment, therefore making this unavailable to those parents living with CPVA. Such limitations allow for the CPVA behaviour not only to escalate, as the child moves into adolescence, but also to become entrenched. Finally, what is clearly evident is that children do not wait until adolescence to display or engage in CPVA, the indicative age for CPVA behaviours remains under 10 years of age. This in itself highlights the necessity to rethink current policies that continue to argue CPVA is an adolescent concern, as this fundamental flaw restricts provision of sustained effective proactive support for families, who experience CPVA within their home.

**Section 4: Let's Talk About: What causes children to behave this way**

This section considers if CPVA behaviour is a facet of a defined SEND condition such as those outlined within the Diagnostic and Statistical Manual of Mental Disorders, (DSM-V 5th Edition). IN doing so this section highlights how the potential for CPVA occurrence is a known aspect for some behavioural special educational needs, this section therefore argues that the current status quo of identifying children via an Educational Health Care Plan, in need of support, wholly fails those children, who 'manage' in school but not at home, due to emotional regulation difficulties. This section highlights the relationship between emotional regulation as an internalised and externalised behaviour that can impact on a Looked After or Previously Looked After[6] child or a child with SEND, leading to displays of CPVA. This section points to reasons why CPVA can become entrenched or can escalate, as a consequence of being overlooked. Furthermore, this section notes that current studies correlating parenting with CPVA overlook therapeutic parenting, an essential aspect of family life for those with a Looked After or Previously Looked After[7] child or a child with SEND. Likewise, family typologies may enable research to be focused on CPVA in specific groups of families, but this does not reflect the internal and external influences upon children and young people, in a more technological age, that has been seen by many as the most powerful influence on children's mental health and wellbeing at this time. Where internal and external impact is a prominent indicator of CPVA, how children and young people engage with their world, or perceive their world externally, is an essential component of developing intervention approaches. This section supports the argument that there is an indicative need to address Adverse Childhood Experiences in any future studies of CPVA. More concerningly, this section highlights how, for

---

[6] including children who are adopted, living with family members (Special Guardianship or Kinship).
[7] including children who are adopted, living with family members (Special Guardianship or Kinship).

many children, the reality not being recognised to meet the requirements for an EHCP, leaves the child and subsequently their family without the support the child requires.

**Section 5: Let's Talk About: The real cost of living with CPVA**

This section provides substantive argument for early intervention as a cost-effective approach for supporting families living with CPVA, from both an economic position and an emotional wellbeing stance. Within this section the cost of living with CPVA for families is identified as both direct and indirect, falling under two overarching areas. The first area is that of economic cost to the family and society, associated with repair and replacement of items or structural needs; alongside the economic cost of loss of employment, restricted employment or reduced employment opportunities, that impacts directly onto the household income. Such impact can then lead to the indirect economic position, whereby these families are left with little alternative options that to seek 'state welfare support' via benefit payments. There is also the additional cost of support services for families with reference to policing, health and social care, alongside education, in much the same way as the costs that are incurred in any domestic violence relationship. Within this section it is argued that in order to help address these potential escalating costs early intervention is essential, to enable these parent/ carers to continue in their employment and to be able to participate in career advancement, should they wish to do so, without restriction. Whilst in the short term, the cost of intervention may excessive, the long-term outcome is cost effective in helping sustain the families economic position; this is achieved through the reduction of both the direct and indirect costs to family and society. It would therefore be prudent and cost effective to retain the family unit successfully, rather than allow the family unit to struggle or live in 'crisis', given that Kanne and Mazurek (2010) stated *aggressive behaviour is a significant predictor of out of home placements among children and young adults with intellectual disabilities;* a factor also noted by Selwyn *et al* (2014). There are existing policies, legislation and practice indicators to provide the support these families need at a time when they need this support; however, it appears that this is a rhetorical position and in the real world these families do not benefit from such policies, legislation or practice, a position that requires immediate attention.

**Section 6: Let's Talk About: Who supports families living with CPVA**

This section reflects current support available and the parental/ carer experience of seeking support when living with CPVA, as a multi-agency provision. Listening to parent/ carers is essential if any support is to be effective and including the parent/ carer experience as a fundamental basis from which support systems should evolve. It is evident from the responses that the parent/carers, participating within the 2018 CPVA survey, have made attempts to access support without success. Whilst some support has been good, much has not been effective or supportive to parent/carer and their child/ children. This section highlights that to support families effectively and efficiently all professionals, irrespective of background, need to understand what CPVA is. There is a wide held definition currently employed that determines all CPVA to be intentional, yet the majority of parent/carers within this study (also within previous studies such as that of Thorley and Coates 2017c) argue this does not apply to their child, or their family, or their reality. This section highlights that despite four decades of research reporting, there continues to be a myriad of responses from professionals to parent/ carers; when they seek help and support for their child who is engaging in CPVA, to them themselves as a parent/ carer and towards members of the family, living within the same household. Furthermore, the majority of effective support and interventions appear to be provided by the voluntary/ charity sector, rather than statutory provision, or has been privately funded by families. This raises concerns about how statutory service professionals engage with families seeking help, and why the least support and least effective interventions are those the Statutory Service professionals provide. Within this section argument is made that there is a need to recognise that CPVA can be perceived by professionals via their own professional 'lens'; a lens that can add bias, misunderstanding, prejudice and presumption about the child, the parent/ carer and the family.

**Section 7: Let's Talk About: What Families living with CPVA suggests happens next**

This section presents what parent/ carers living with CPVA feel works and what does not. This section reflects on training offered to date to parent/ carers responding within the 2018 CPVA survey, that points to a fragmented ad hoc approach, which is nether helpful or effective. Training offered to families is dependent on where the parent/carer lives and what is available in the area, rather than what is needed. Furthermore, many parent/ carers wait unreasonable lengthy times to receive this training due to funding indicators. The impact of developing discussion about the reality of CPVA, across society, for families is viewed with a mixed response by parent/ carers responses. For many parent/ carers opening up discussion has been helpful and reduced feelings of guilt about being 'to blame' for their child's behaviour, enabling them to feel less alone and supporting them when seeking help. Alternatively, for others media coverage has sensationalised CPVA in unhelpful ways, leading to advice being offered by anyone and everyone, irrespective of that persons experience, knowledge or understanding of CPVA. This section outlines the suggestions parent/ carers indicate would promote good practice, particularly from professionals, in order to help other parent/ carers who find themselves living with CPVA. In this way this section outlines 'where next' and points to a preference for action rather than more discussion. In summary this section points to nine suggestions that parent/carers highlight is needed in order to support them and their family collectively.

**Section 8: Let's Talk About: Reflecting on CPVA**

The 2018 CPVA survey looked to view the respondents as experts by experience, recognising as such, that they have offered a valuable insight to their lived experience. An underlying question that has to be considered with reference to the parent/ carers responding, is in relation to the level of their knowledge, experience and analysis of the causes of their child's challenging, violent and aggressive behaviour. This section recognises Scourfield's (2009) position, that experts by experience are only 'experts' of their area and of their specific lived experience; in this way it is recognised that such experiences are personalised to individuals and may not resonate with others. However, given the nature of the questions posed, such depth of detail on a larger scale may be difficult to ascertain. This section recognises that across all participant parent/carers there is broad agreement on what constitutes violence and aggression, however there continues to be questions around motivation and underlying issues that lead to violence and aggression. One aim of this study was to consider if the widely used definition *'Any harmful act by a child, whether physical, psychological or financial, which is intended to gain power and control over a parent or carer'* (Cottrell 2004) was considered appropriate by those parent/ carers taking part in the survey. The purpose of exploring how CPVA is defined from the parent/ carer position was not to prove Cottrell's definition to be misleading or incorrect; rather, it was to develop discussions that have been increasing across social media, and included into research reports; that point to the definition being problematic for some parent/ carers when discussing their child. This section outlines parental/ carer responses and offers suggestions towards their views on a preferred definition. In this way, what transpired, is that the global definition currently used does reflect CPVA behaviour by those children who do intend to engage in CPVA and opt for this approach in their behaviour, especially for those children seeking to have control over their parent/ carer. Similarly, the global definition provided this study, with the opportunity to recognise the differences between those children who actively engage in CPVA with intention, to those who displayed CPVA without intention. This was an important distinction, more than two-thirds of parent/ carers, responding to the 2018 CPVA survey, stated that their child's display of CPVA was without intention, therefore the global definition of CPVA did not resonate with these parent/ carers or reflect their child's behaviour.  This means, that the current practice of identifying children who engage in CPVA, as a collective group of children, irrespective of the child's individual history or health indicators, fails to meet the needs of the child and by association the needs of the family. This section argues that this is an essential nuance of wording, recognising that there is a need to separate those children who ***intend to engage*** in CPVA, as distinctively a different group of children, to those children who ***display CPVA unintentionally***. This section suggests that with continued developing knowledge, relating to the underlying triggers and causes of child violence, aggression and challenging behaviour; it is elemental to recognise the distinct difference in CPVA with or without intention. This will then inform professional response, an argument also posited by Holt (2016) who argues that our definition of Child to Parent Violence shapes how we understand it and subsequently respond to it. Separating the two distinctive ways, in which children demonstrate CPVA, enables effective support to be provided. Furthermore, whilst there is growing concern about the increasing numbers of children employing CPVA as a behaviour, there is a need to recognise the impact of the technological world. Emerging new technologies encourage data and information sharing, which has been an invaluable informal support network for many parent/ carers, but this also opens up the issue of CPVA to a wider society overall.  In this way, emerging technologies and support groups online may also be instrumental in these increasing number of CPVA numbers reported; for example, within social media such as Twitter and Facebook parents living with CPVA are able to connect with other parents, in ways that were previously unavailable. This in itself will encourage more open discussion of living with CPVA, CPVA causes and CPVA behaviours. It is therefore unknown if CPVA is increasing, or if awareness of CPVA is increasing, or if a combination of both is occurring.

# Section 2: Let's Talk About
# Families living with CPVA

**Indicators and predictors: What kinds of Families experience CPVA**

There is a myriad of literature pointing to a range of family types that are at higher risk of CPVA occurrence, as outlined by Gallagher (2008). Gallagher acknowledged there were specific family typologies where CPVA appears more prevalent including: child's gender (more boys than girls) and mothers as the 'victim' (with a slighter higher incidence for single mothers or those with a history of domestic violence within the family household[8]). For the 2018 CPVA survey family units and households were identified by two basic premises; firstly, the adult relationship to the child and secondly whether the adults were in a couple relationship or single parents. This approach enabled a more generic collection of data and allowed for 'couples' who were birth parents, adopters, kinship carers, Special Guardians (SGO[9]), foster parents, or blended families and so forth to be included. In this way the focus was not so much on the parent but rather interrogated the parent's relationship to the child that was displaying CPVA. Additionally, data generated enabled those participating to be representative of family households calculated within national statistics for the UK. Within the UK the Office of National Statistics (ONS) records family unit types with and without dependent children. Those family units with dependent children are recorded as lone mothers (rather than single parents per se) alongside four family sub-group couples[10]. It is interesting that there is no provision for 'lone father family with dependent children'; whilst proportionally lone father families may be a minority, dependent children can potentially be overlooked if not included as a family 'type' within National Statistical records. The current total of family types including sub-groups, living within the UK in 2017 and reported by ONS is outlined within Chart 2

---

[8] Similar to the findings of Cottrell and Monk (2004)
[9] SGO: Special Guardianship Order
[10] civil partner cohabiting, opposite sex cohabiting, married couple and same sex cohabiting

**Chart 2: family typologies with children in household (counted by 1,000s)**

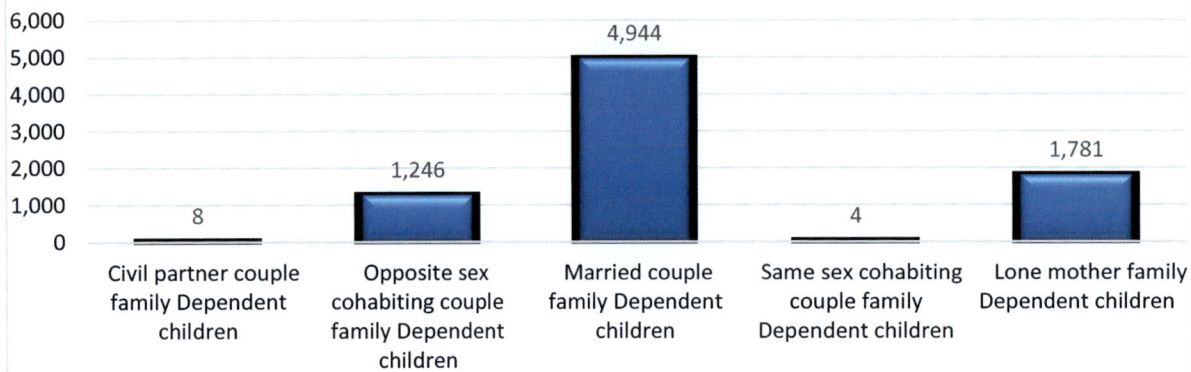

|  |  |
|----------|-------|
| Civil partner couple family Dependent children | 8 |
| Opposite sex cohabiting couple family Dependent children | 1,246 |
| Married couple family Dependent children | 4,944 |
| Same sex cohabiting couple family Dependent children | 4 |
| Lone mother family Dependent children | 1,781 |

Within its report for 2017, the Office of National Statistics highlights that the largest growing number of families at this time is that of blended families; although statistically there continues to be more married couple families with dependent children than any other sub-group (as highlighted within Chart 2). The growing number of blended families is an important consideration when discussing CPVA prevalence or risk, in that whilst it is recognised a wide range of prevalent factors increase the risk of CPVA, a substantial number of these point to adolescents within non-traditional families (of married mother and father). Such pointers towards non-traditional families go on to note that there is a higher incidence of CPVA prevalence within blended families and single parent families (Kennair and Mellor, 2007; Ibabe et al, 2013; Ibabe, 2016). However, the diversity within family units with dependent children reflects limited information regarding family sub-groups, in that they record the here and now rather than how the family unit become so[11]. In this way neither the sub-group in itself, or the discussion made by ONS relating to blended families, include details of how the 'blended family' developed. Whilst there tends to be agreement that a blended family is one that *'consists of two adults, the child or children that they have had together, and one or more children that they have had with previous partners'* (Cambridge Dictionary, 2018 n.p) this provides little insight into how the family became blended. This means there is no indicator of whether or not the adults include parents who were previously single parents, or part of a traditional 'parent' family, or a same gender parent family and so forth. Such aspects are important if it is accepted that there is a clear shift away from more 'traditional' married

---

[11] insomuch as the Office of National Statistics (2017) reflect family unit typologies at that period of time only

couple families to that of a blended family given that the risk of CPVA incidence can occurring increases within blended families.

In contrast to the suggestions made, regarding blended families and single parents, the participant responses generated within the CPVA 2018 survey reflected predominantly more 'couples' than 'single parents', at 75% and 25% respectively. It could be argued that on the basis of these findings there are significantly more 'couple' families that will experience CPVA than single parents, a finding that is contradictory to previous suggestions of a higher risk within single parent households. Alternatively, it may be that the couple respondents were part of a blended family and therefore remain situated in a higher risk category of experiencing CPVA. Furthermore, this may be based on simple statistics, in that across the UK there are statistically far more 'couple' relationships (as shown in Chart 2) than those of single parenthood; therefore, there are far more families with children who live as couples than there are single parents. This therefore may account for why statistically speaking it would be expected more couples will experience CPVA than single parent households, in terms of actual number of families living with CPVA. Whilst discussing CPVA prevalence and risk, within single parent and blended families, Ibabe (2016, p.1538) proposed this was *"where these families have a higher level of distress and limited resources to address the adolescent stage of the child"*. In contradiction to these suggestions by Ibabe (*ibid*) no couple participants, responding within the CPVA 2018 survey (representing 75% of the responses received), were part of a blended family, yet they were all living with CPVA as indicated in Chart 3.

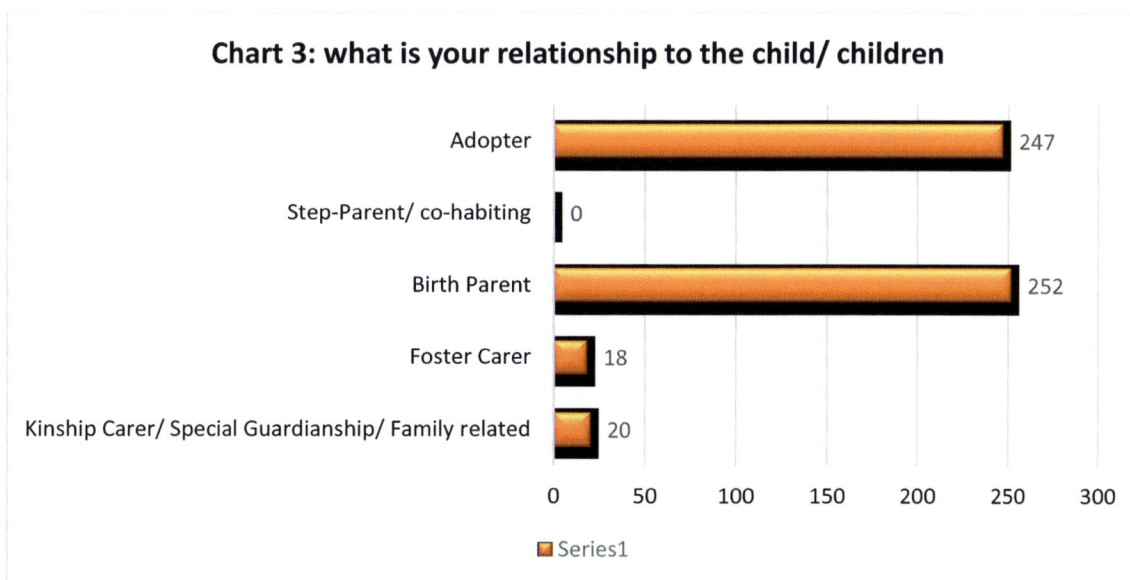

**Chart 3: what is your relationship to the child/ children**

|  |  |
|---|---|
| Adopter | 247 |
| Step-Parent/ co-habiting | 0 |
| Birth Parent | 252 |
| Foster Carer | 18 |
| Kinship Carer/ Special Guardianship/ Family related | 20 |

(x-axis: 0, 50, 100, 150, 200, 250, 300)

Series1

21

What is noteworthy, within discussions about family 'groups' and increased risk of CPVA occurrence, is how these families are perceived from the adult position, rather than the child position. This is an essential nuance if developing understanding of CPVA and establishing prevalence or risk of CPVA occurring within specific families. Whist the current definition recognises a blended family is *'a family that consists of two adults, ….'* (Cambridge Dictionary, 2018 n.p.) it does not clarify the position of the children within the family. In this way the definition offered fails to recognise those families with children who are 'Looked After' (LAC) or have been 'Previously Looked After' (PLAC); irrespective of whether the child is part of a Foster family, Adopted family, Special Guardianship family or Kinship family. Deconstructing current understanding of what a blended family means and reconstructing this, to take account of children within that family, provides a more realistic appraisal of heightened risk factors or prevalence of CPVA occurring. Changing the narrative to interrogate family-child positions within the family, for those families living with CPVA, illustrates how children who are 'Looked After' (LAC) or have been 'Previously Looked After' (PLAC) are part of all family 'types'. As detailed within the participant responses 75% were a 'couple' family (404 participants); however, their relationship to the child/ children in the household varied. Moving the analysis to consider the relationship between 'parent/carer' couples and their children underlined how varied these relationships can be, that enabled a partition of four further sub-groups, within couple responses, to be identified as:

- couple with birth child/ children displaying CPVA,
- couple with adopted child/ children displaying CPVA,
- couple with a family relationship to the child/ children displaying CPVA (Kinship or Special Guardian parental roles) and
- couple with foster child/ children displaying CPVA.

If applying the Office of National Statistics criteria of couples with dependent children all of the participating couple families would be included; however, within those responses received from parents living with CPVA, only 43% identified the children as their 'birth children', as reflected within chart 3. Whilst birth parents represented more families than any other family group, those family groups where the child was not a birth child were the majority of respondents, if combining all non-birth families collectively. This reiterates the importance of recognising the position of the child within the household and the need for deconstructing current definitions of what a blended family is. Applying a wider definition to 'blended family' that allows for the child position as the 'blended' aspect rather than the adult position allows for single parent responses and couple parents response to be combined and changes the responses from 'blended families' from 0% as outlined within Chart 3 to 53% as shown in Chart 4:

## Chart 4: parent-child relationship (sub-group)

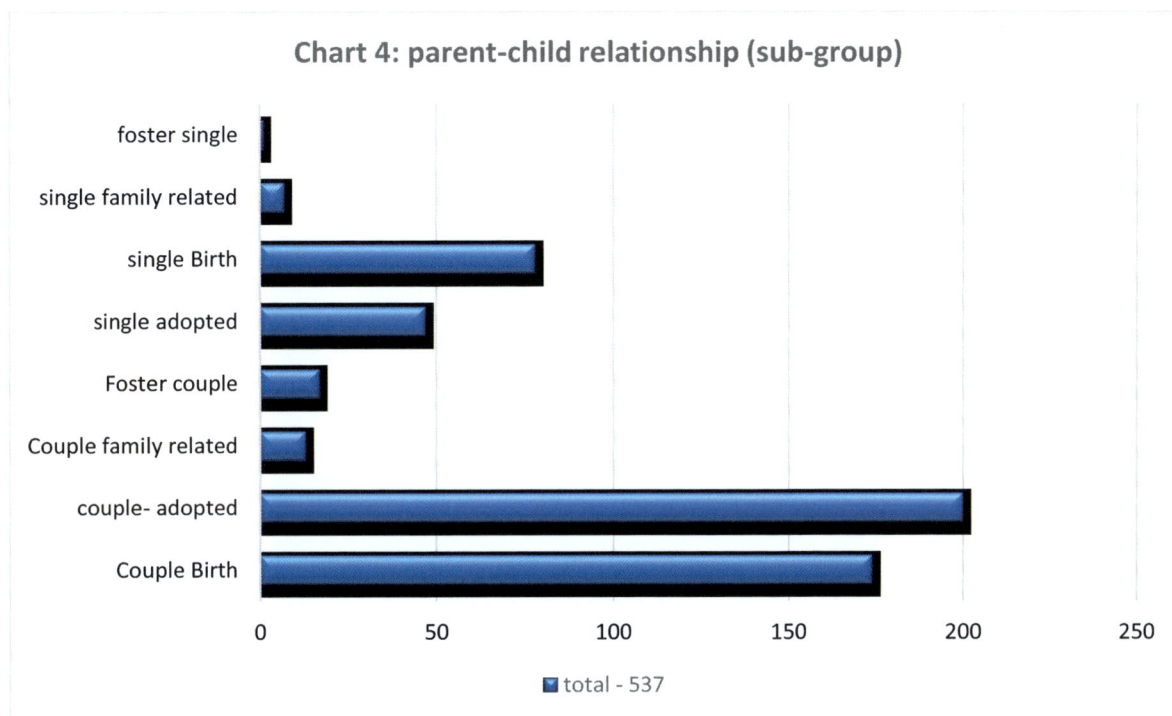

Recalculating relationship responses, via the child's and 'parent' figures, rather than the adult to adult relationship, expands the notion of a 'blended family'; and in this way recognises all adopter families, foster care families and Kinship/ Special Guardian families living with CPVA, irrespective of the cohabiting or single status of the parents themselves. Applying this approach, to the responses received, supports previous suggestions of a higher prevalence and risk in blended families, as well as higher levels of CPVA reported by Adopters, Kinship carers, Special Guardians as well as Single parents. More importantly, current suggestions of increased risk and prevalence of CPVA within blended or single parent families, do not elaborate on any details of how these families became so; for example, is single parenthood due to partner parental death, separation or divorce, all of which are indicators of Adverse Childhood Experiences[12]. Acknowledging how blended and single parent families evolved

---

[12] The Adverse Childhood Experiences Study (**ACE Study**) is a research **study** conducted by the American health maintenance organization Kaiser Permanente and the Centers for Disease Control and Prevention (1995-1997) leading to a wide range of

would facilitate interrogation of any increased risk or prevalence of CPVA to be recognised, that may well be a subsequence of Adverse Childhood Experience (ACE), rather than a consequence of family type. Additionally, reconfiguring data generated, regarding 'blended children', provides support for suggestions of a higher risk of CPVA occurrence by children with higher levels of Adverse Childhood Experience indicators, irrespective of where they now reside. Of those respondents within the survey 49.5% were adoptive couples, 3.2% were kinship carers/ Special Guardians and 4.2% were Foster Care couples; thereby confirming previous suggestions that children who are 'Looked After' (LAC) or have been 'Previously Looked After' (PLAC) present a higher risk of engaging in CPVA than their peers. However, this increased risk did not reflect the findings for single parent households. As detailed previously, 25% of respondents were single parent households (133 participants), of which 58.6% were parents with birth child/ children. The findings for 'single parent-birth child' is the highest group of parents experiencing CPVA, for single parent households participating in this 2018 CPVA survey, which contrasts to the findings of couple parents living with CPVA (in couple parents 'adopters' were the highest family group experiencing CPVA). Within single parents, living with CPVA, single adopters were more than 20% lower (at 35%) than single parents with birth child/ children, experiencing and living with CPVA. Moreover, if calculating single adopters, single foster carers and single Kinship/Special Guardians collectively, who were living with and experiencing CPVA, as a blended-child family, they remained a lower response group to that of single birth-parent. This highlights the need to consider risk against proportionate representation, of the collective numbers of families within society, for example whilst single parent-birth child is highlighted as a higher risk category, they would also account for more single parent families within the UK overall, to that of single parent-adopted child (or single parent Kinship/ Special Guardian or single parent-Foster child). Following this position, it can be suggested that if being a single parent does increase the risk of CPVA occurrence, it could be anticipated this would involve more single parent-birth children, than that of single parent-adoptive child for example.

The importance of reconstructing blended families, to recognise 'blended-children' as a family type, not only enables children who are 'Looked After' (LAC) or have been 'Previously Looked

---

publications which are listed at: http://www.theannainstitute.org/ACE%20STUDY%20FINDINGS.html. This study has been replicated internationally and is widely recognised for predicting future indicators for children as they progress to adulthood, for example see the The Public Health Wales NHS Report (2015) at: http://www.cph.org.uk/wp-content/uploads/2016/01/ACE-Report-FINAL-E.pdf ; and Liverpool Johns Moore University (2016) in their study from Hertfordshire, Luton and Northhamptonshire available at: http://www.cph.org.uk/wp-content/uploads/2016/05/Adverse-Childhood-Experiences-in-Hertfordshire-Luton-and-Northamptonshire-FINAL_compressed.pdf

After' (PLAC)[13] to be identified as a child who maybe at a higher risk of engaging in CPVA behaviour, but also allows for consideration to be given to any previous family they may have resided with, prior to their current home environment. This approach then allows for recognition of any impact of Adverse Childhood Experiences to be considered, acknowledged and identified. Adopting an Adverse Childhood Experience basis, from which to consider prevalence and risk from the child's position, instead of highlighting current family unit 'type', may provide specific detailed indicators about those children who are at an increased risk of displaying CPVA; irrespective of where they now reside, thereby helping to provide explanation of why some children, who are currently Looked After or have been Previously Looked After, display CPVA behaviours.  Furthermore, this would then enable the child's previous experiences to be fully acknowledged, as a factor in any CPVA reported, irrespective of where they now reside; for example, any previous childhood experience that included the child living with domestic violence, parents who engage in substance misuse, being neglected by parents or parental imprisonment. Implementing a full history of the child's experiences, that include pre-natal impact[14] and post-natal experiences[15], helps to explain why CPVA may not present initially, but later in childhood when living with a different family household, including a family household that is not biologically related to the child, acknowledging what Van der Kolk (2014) described as 'the body keeps the score'.

Reconstructing a wider definition to 'blended families' enables distinct sub-groups to be identified (by families that include children with SEND or children who are 'Looked After' or have been 'Previously Looked After'), that in turn can support previous indicators of an increased risk of CPVA occurrence within non-traditional families. Such recognition of sub-groups within family types then helps support debate and previous studies that acknowledge a significantly higher risk of CPVA occurring for Foster Carers, Adopters and Kinship Carers. However, these studies to date have continued to overlook children with SEND engaging in CPVA behaviours, within any family unit type.  Recognising the relationship between CPVA and SEND is the most under-researched aspect of CPVA to date, yet many children who display CPVA, from all family typologies, are diagnosed with SEND; not only SEND as such but these children are often diagnosed with co-morbid conditions, particularly those children who are Looked After or Previously Looked After. CPVA however should not be perceived as a

---

[13] Irrespective of whether they now reside in lone mother families, civil partner couple families, opposite sex cohabiting families, married couple families or same sex cohabiting couple families.
[14] as employed for example in Neurosequential approaches (Perry 1998, 2006)
[15] As employed for example in the ACE studies (1995-1997)

behaviour trait of only those children with SEND, or Looked After Children, or Previously Looked After Children, as highlighted by Wilcox and Pooley (2015). Wilcox and Pooley (ibid) conducted their study of CPV across several European Countries, identifying that CPVA was evident across all family group types, a position that Robinson (2010 p.2) had previously highlighted within the Churchill funded study on Teen Violence Against Parents (TVAP); in which they asserted that … *"this issue spans both genders, the entire range of family structures and all income brackets. It can be found in deprived and affluent neighbourhoods; crossing many cultural and international boundaries"*. Similarly, Broadhead and Francis (2015) warn against seeing CPVA by any definition or terminology applied as a particular family typology, or a specific group of children or young people, be this by age, socio-demography or other defining characteristic (within which Special Educational Needs or Disability, Looked After Children or Previously Looked After Children could be viewed as a defining characteristic or label). They acknowledge that there are pre-disposing factors that may increase the risk of CPVA within family units, but they are not determinants of CPVA.

Taking a broader perspective of CPVA occurrence, beyond the basic construction of family typologies, includes suggestions that link CPVA to specific aspects of social, economic and cultural grouping. Ibabe (2016) focused on academic failure, noting lower socio-economic status or disadvantaged children reflected a higher prevalence of CPVA. However, Gallagher (2008) emphasised that such indicators should not define why CPVA occurs, nor which family units CPVA occurs in, arguing that CPVA affects family units of all types who are experiencing a range of circumstances and that *"There is NEVER just one cause for any complex behaviour and 'explanations' of someone's behaviour may be in terms of the individual (both genetic/ biological and past experience), the family and the wider society. All of these play a part."* (ibid.). Such indications recognise the problems of trying to establishing CPVA 'types', in that whilst CPVA exists across all family types, statistically there continues to be more families within society who do not live with CPVA than do live with CPVA. This does not diminish the impact of CPVA for those families who are experiencing CPVA from their children, rather it raises questions about suggestions that point to specific family type. Pointing to a family or child 'type' can be unhelpful when interrogating why CPVA occurs, unless also establishing the child's position within that family household. Further difficulties arise when focusing on the family who are known to be living with CPVA, in that much CPVA is not reported or recorded. Therefore, indicators of prevalence rely on families who do seek help, rather than those who do not. In this way it could be argued that these family 'types' who are identified at risk of higher prevalence of CPVA are misidentified; insomuch as they represent families more likely to seek help rather than families at higher risk. It is also possible that those families who do not fit into known family types seek 'privately funded' support and intervention and consequently remain unknown.

Building on from Thorley and Coates (2017a, b and c) one of the fundamental areas that were noted for further exploration related to 'other' children in the family household. This is an underlying important aspect of family cohesion when living with CPVA. There appears to be limited research that outlines how many children overall were in the household where CPVA was displayed, or how many other children within the household also display CPVA. Indicators generated from previous studies would suggest that children who live with CPVA, rather than are displaying CPVA, are subjected to similar childhood experiences as those children who live with domestic violence. Domestic violence in the home tends to be viewed by society as adult to adult violence, yet CPVA introduces violence into the home environment (irrespective of the age of the child engaging in CPVA). This means that children living within homes where CPVA is displayed are residing with domestic violence, albeit not that of adult to adult but violence nevertheless. Following this indicator, it therefore does not appear to be unrealistic to anticipate those siblings living with, rather than engaging in, CPVA are impacted upon by this form of domestic violence. Of greater concern CPVA can also include 'Sibling violence', or child on child violence and abuse and as Caspi (2011, p.207) noted this is a much under researched concern *"In my professional practice, I have observed sibling violence is frequently accompanied by child to parent violence, although this co-existence, has not to my knowledge been studied."* Research to date for CPVA acknowledges sibling abuse may occur[16] but does not appear to interrogate this as an area within CPVA, rather sibling violence tends to be viewed separately, yet sibling safety is of prime concern for parents who are subject to CPVA. For this reason, within the CPVA Survey 2018 information gathered, data included how many children under the age of 18 years resided within the family home, as shown in chart 5

---

[16] Sibling abuse, similar to CPVA, is a much under-reported concern within families in that research to date for CPVA acknowledge sibling abuse may occur but do not interrogate this as an independent area, nor do they provide depth of impact of sibling abuse upon siblings. Sibling abuse is noted for example within Home Office (2015), Coogan (2011). As early as 2000 Flowers included CPVA and sibling abuse within the umbrella of domestic crimes alongside domestic violence, a discussion also noted in Lamanna et al (2016) that pointed to the impact on children from living with domestic violence, not only that demonstrated by adults in the home.

## Chart 5: Number of children within the household overall

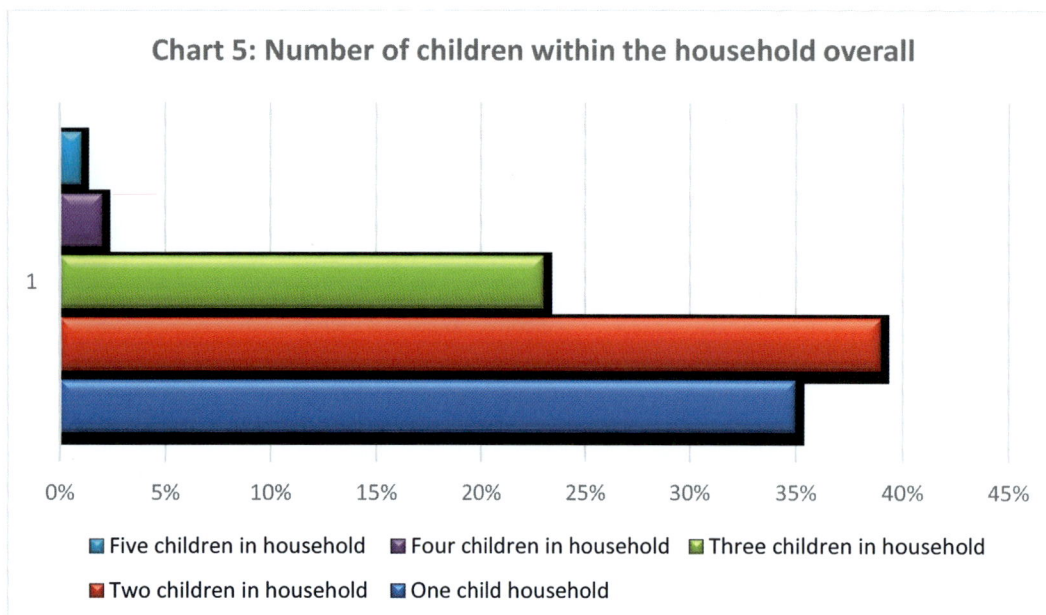

Legend:
- Five children in household
- Four children in household
- Three children in household
- Two children in household
- One child household

Thorley and Coates (2017 a, b and c) noted within their reports the impact on siblings and the safety of siblings was the main concern for parents participating in their survey. Furthermore, parents' experience a conundrum when attempting to manage both the CPVA relationship, as well as their relationship with other children in the home. Within Selwyn *et al's* (2014) study they noted that for those parents, where adoption breakdown had occurred, violence to parents and siblings was the main reason for children leaving home prematurely (80%) and hence adoption/placement breakdown. The concomitant phenomenon for siblings living with CPVA is at this time unknown, however, living with adverse childhood experiences is well documented within the ACE study. The potential for increased co-morbidity health indicators, for siblings living with CPVA, therefore supports the necessity of equipping families to manage CPVA, should this occur, as an early intervention rather than waiting until such time CPVA escalates. The basis from which intervention, approaches, strategies and therapies should be developed needs to account for all members of the family impacted by CPVA, including siblings. It is for this reason the CPVA survey specifically included sibling data. The participant response reflects a range of family groups with reference to the number of children and young people (CYP) within the home environment as detailed in chart 6.

## Chart 6: Number of children within the home where CPVA is a concern, by family sub-group

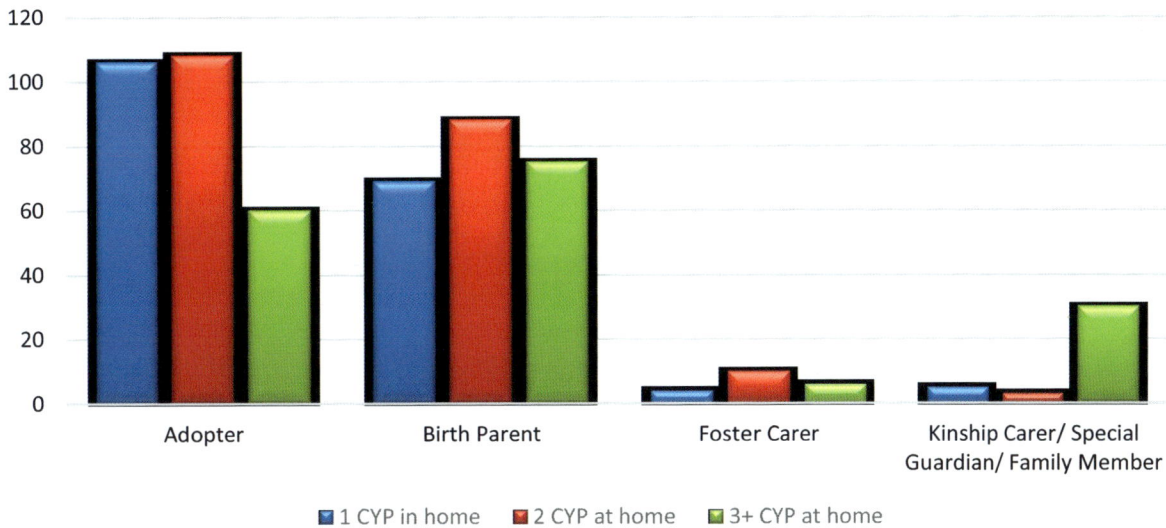

Having established how many children under the age of 18 lived within the family home, participants were asked to indicate the age of those children displaying CPVA. This information then provided the basis for statistical analysis that determined how many of the children within the home were engaging in CPVA, compared to how many children or young people lived within the home overall. What is evident within the findings, illustrated in chart 6, is that collectively families living with one adopted child or two adopted children are at higher risk of experiencing CPVA, and significantly more so than other family groups where there are one or two children in the home. However, where there are three (or more) children in the home it is those parents living with birth children, or those living with related children (Kinship/ SGOs), who are more at risk of living with CPVA. This highlights why it is crucial to consider the impact of living in a domestic violence household on siblings, when CPVA is displayed, to provide insight into why some children may be returned to 'care' as previously indicated by Selwyn (2014). The focus for parents at this time is not solely attempting to meet the needs of the child displaying CPVA, but to also address the real child protection concerns these children may present to other children within the home. The importance of understanding sibling impact, alongside parent/carer impact, is highlighted within the findings outlined within chart 7

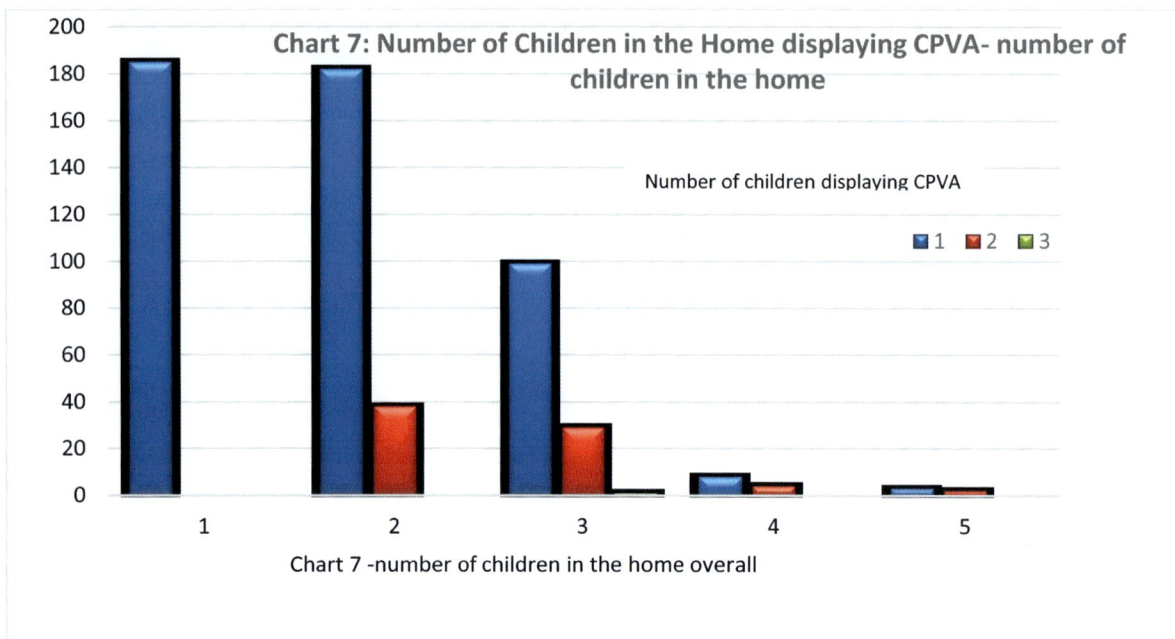

Chart 7: Number of Children in the Home displaying CPVA- number of children in the home

Number of children displaying CPVA

Chart 7 -number of children in the home overall

There were 185 responses from households with one child within the home displaying CPVA, representing 39% of the responses received. However, this means 61% of those responding represent families with more than one child within the home where CPVA occurs. Analysing the findings of responses to the number of children in households, compared to the number of children displaying CPVA, highlights that in those households with more than one child in residence, it is predominantly one child who displays CPVA. This means the other siblings are living in a domestic violence household and are therefore subject to the impact of Adverse Childhood Experiences related to violence within the home. As demonstrated within Chart 7 there were 220 families with 2 children residing at home, of which 83% experienced CPVA from one child. These parent/ carers who are seeking to manage the CPVA behaviour, will also need to ensure there is limited risk of 'sibling violence' arising or occurring. Furthermore, as a form of domestic abuse, these children who are witnessing CPVA within their home could be said to be 'at risk', in much the same way as children who live with domestic violence between adults are 'at risk'. This can be seen within the Adoption and Children Act 2002 Section 120, that amended the definition of harm outlined within Section 31 (9) of the Children Act 1989, to enable 'harm' to include 'impairment suffered from seeing or hearing the ill-treatment of another'. This is a significant legal position that could, in reality, enable Children's Services across England and Wales to remove children from the family home as a consequence of witnessing CPVA, by recognising this as a form of domestic abuse. There are no indicators to suggest such action has been taken, for which the only explanation feasible appears to be that within the UK, CPVA specifically may not be viewed as a form of domestic violence (a factor also noted by Condry and Miles, 2014). However, there are indicators to point to children who have been placed in 'care' because of the CPVA they display. It can therefore be argued that in these circumstances parent/ carers are left with little option, other than to place children who engage in CPVA into the care of the Local Authority, because of the risk of 'harm' for any siblings witnessing these behaviours.

Siblings at risk of harm is notable where more than one child engages in CPVA within the household, due to the impact of CPVA not being isolated to one child only in multi-child households. Responses indicated that 17% of families experienced CPVA from both children in two child households. Moreover, 128 families participating in the study lived with 3 children, of which 77% of these families experienced CPVA from one child, with 2 children exposed to the impact of CPVA as a form of domestic violence. In addition, in the remaining 23% of families (where 3 children reside) 2 children displayed CPVA, leaving the one child not engaging in CPVA extremely vulnerable within the home, both as witness to the violence and as a potential future 'sibling victim'. Becoming a sibling victim of CPVA would arguably place the lone child to be subject to a higher level of potential 'harm', under the Adoption and Children Act 2002 Section 120.  Less than 1% of households with 3 children residing in the home experienced CPVA from all three children; however, this raises further concerns regarding the safety of the parent/carers who are experiencing CPVA from all of the children present.  Within responses received 12 households indicated that four children resided in the home, within which 2/3rds of these families experienced one child engaging in CPVA (witnessed by the remaining three children) and 1/3$^{rd}$ of these families experiencing CPVA from 2 children (witnessed by the remaining two children). Whilst those families with 5 or more children residing at home are in the minority statistically, this can highlight different challenges. Kinship carers and Special Guardians often accept children from 'kin' into their home, frequently these families will also have children of their own. There were 8 families responding who indicated 5 children lived within the family home, of these families 60% experienced CPVA from one child, whilst 40% experienced CPVA from 2 children. This highlights the need to investigate more fully the impact upon siblings, particularly if some of the children within the home are a 'blended aspect', with regard to how this relates to CPVA experienced by those parent/carers with multiple children's needs to protect.

**Section Summary**

This section highlights how and why family types alone, do not provide sufficient information regarding increased risk of CPVA occurrence. This section also argues that there is a need for reconstructing how society perceives blended families, arguing there is a need to expand this definition in order to include the child's position, not solely the adult position. More importantly, there is a real need to recognise CPVA as a form of domestic abuse, particularly where more than one child resides within the family home. This chapter points to fundamental areas of CPVA impact that are under researched and underrepresented, within discussions of CPVA to date. The first is that of children with SEND who are significantly overlooked in current trends focusing on CPVA. The second is that of siblings who are exposed to potential 'harm' whilst living with violence in home environment. These factors are essential if CPVA is to be explored and support for families is to be offered. Furthermore, some SEND diagnosis can be related to pre-natal influences, for example Foetal Alcohol Spectrum Disorders if there is maternal substance abuse; which would point to Adverse Childhood Experiences as a risk factor of CPVA occurring. Following pre-natal possibilities, violence within the home is also recognised as an Adverse Childhood Experience and whilst this is more readily discussed as adult to adult, recognition of child to adult violence needs to be accounted for within discussions of domestic violence. In this way, this chapter highlights the necessity of recognising Adverse Childhood Experiences within any study of children who engage in CPVA behaviours as an influencing factor; thereby enabling any discussion of CPVA risk to include both pre and post- natal factors, that may impact upon the child directly as an area of Adversity within their Childhood (ACE). Explanation for how and why single parents become so is also important, to allow for full consideration to be made with reference to Adverse Childhood Experiences, for example single parent widowhood, due to the death of a parent. This information, once generated can then be applied to the types of CPVA behaviours a child's displays to identify patterns or correlations should they exist.

# Section 3. Let's Talk About -
# Age-stage expectations and behaviour.

One of the difficulties encountered when trying to determine what behaviour constitutes CPVA is establishing exactly why the behaviour is different to any normative or cultural expectation, for example 'toddler tantrums'. Toddler tantrums are recognised as an age-stage developmental norm, therefore differentiating between anticipated norms and something beyond this is not always straight-forward. For many families it is the 'feeling' that something is not as it should be or is beyond what they expected and anticipated. In this way, the notion of CPVA becomes subjective and personalised; however, such concerns should not be dismissed as a reflection of 'over-anxious' parent/ carers. Ullman and Straus (2003) highlighted similar difficulties when determining what behaviours equate to CPVA, suggesting that some studies excluded younger children due to difficulties in categorising the level of physical injury sustained by parent/ carer's. Such positions argue that physical injury sustained by parent/ carers, as a consequence of CPVA caused by young children, would be minor or slight and therefore should not be perceived as CPVA. However, this approach discounts the emotional impact of CPVA for parent/ carers, as well as the physical pain that can be associated with CPVA involving younger children, as indicated by Ulman and Straus (2003: 42) who assert CPVA from children as young as three should be included as *"it can be assumed that a child who kicks or bites a parent wants the parent to experience pain"*. This is of importance because their study is regularly quoted as showing 18% of children are violent to parents. Additionally, Parentline (2008) noted 60% of the calls they received were for verbal aggression, not physical aggression, therefore these parent/ carers would not have significant physical injury.  Adopting a position of excluding younger children as age-stage behaviours can lead to the focus towards teens; thereby supporting suggestions that CPVA is more frequently displayed during adolescence. Such discussion led Martinez *et al* (2015) to propose the difference underpinning CPVA, to any normative age-stage behaviour, was based in an 'exercise of power' in adolescents, rather than the anticipated normative behaviour traits displayed by adolescents during their teen years. Such suggestions focus on the power relationship outlined within definitions of CPVA currently used, leading to discernment between normative expectations of teens as part of their developing maturity and independence, a position also noted by Kuay *et al* (2017).  The majority of publications highlight CPVA as most prominent during teen years, going onto to suggest the occurrence of this behaviour reduces as those teens mature into adulthood (see for example, Ulman & Straus, 2003; Holt, 2013; Condry & Miles, 2014; Ibabe, 2014; Ibabe & Bentler, 2016). Such argument would account for guidance provided by the Home Office (2015, p.3- 1.1) who recognise CPVA as adolescent to parent violence, going onto determine that *Adolescent to parent violence and abuse (APVA) may be referred to as 'adolescent to parent violence (APV)' 'adolescent violence in the home (AVITH)', 'parent abuse', 'child to parent abuse', 'child to parent violence (CPV)', or 'battered parent syndrome*, thereby negating violent or aggressive behaviour by younger children as CPVA. Whilst they do acknowledge that adolescent to parent violence can occur and involve those under 16 years of age (when their Guidance for Domestic Abuse would be relevant), by definition an adolescent is considered to mean older children rather than all children.

Adolescence in itself can be ambiguous in that it can mean when puberty begins such as the 'traditional' age of 13-14 years of age (Silver, 2018), or at 10 years of age if applying the World Health Organisation indicator. However, Sawyer *et al* (2018) argue that *'The ages of 10-24 years are a better fit with the development of adolescents nowadays'* extending UNICEF and the World Health Organisation's suggestion of 10-19 years of age. Nevertheless, as Sawyer *et al* (ibid) point out determining age from a biological perspective is problematic. This is particular relevant when discussing CPVA, insomuch as chronological age does not always reflect developmental age; yet chronological age continues to be the main consideration for determining CPVA behaviour by individual children, particularly those children with SEND. Regardless of the dispute over commencement and duration of adolescence, the major flaw for adopting such indicators when discussing CPVA continues, in that Thorley and Coates (2017a, b and c) pointed to the highest incidence of CPVA occurrence was earlier than adolescence, so much so that adolescence was the lowest age range from the responses they received. Ulman and Straus (2003) noted similar, they highlighted that 1/3$^{rd}$ of their survey group involving 3-5 year olds were violent to a parent over the previous 12 month period, compared to 1:10 for 14-17 year olds during the same period. Selwyn *et al* (2014 p.146) concur and whilst they recognised the hormonal impact of adolescents they also noted that

> *Many parents described a rapid escalation of challenging behaviour in their child, as they approached puberty. Adopters reported that children were on average 11 years old (range 5-17 years, SD 2.9) when difficulties began to escalate. One in five families saw the onset and escalation of difficulties at this time.*

Within their study (*ibid*) they also noted that where the placement had broken down, for adopter parents, the onset tended to be later at average age of 8 years old, compared to those children who were currently within the home environment at an average age of 7 years.  But more importantly for those children no longer within the adoptive home environment, their placement began at an older age than those who were still within the home. What is noted and of particular concern is their reference to those families who report difficulties at an early age (within early years of age 0-5 or between 5-7 years of age); thereby reiterating the indicators of Ullman and Straus (2003). A similar pattern of higher levels of CPVA pre-adolescence was identified within responses for this CPVA survey (2018), reinforcing discussion about CPVA as a 'childhood' concern not just an adolescent concern. The most prevalent age at the time of the 2018 CPVA survey was aged 6-9 years of age collectively, whilst those children aged between 2 years and 10/11 years of age, represent 64% of all children residing in family households where only one child displayed CPVA, as shown in Chart 8.

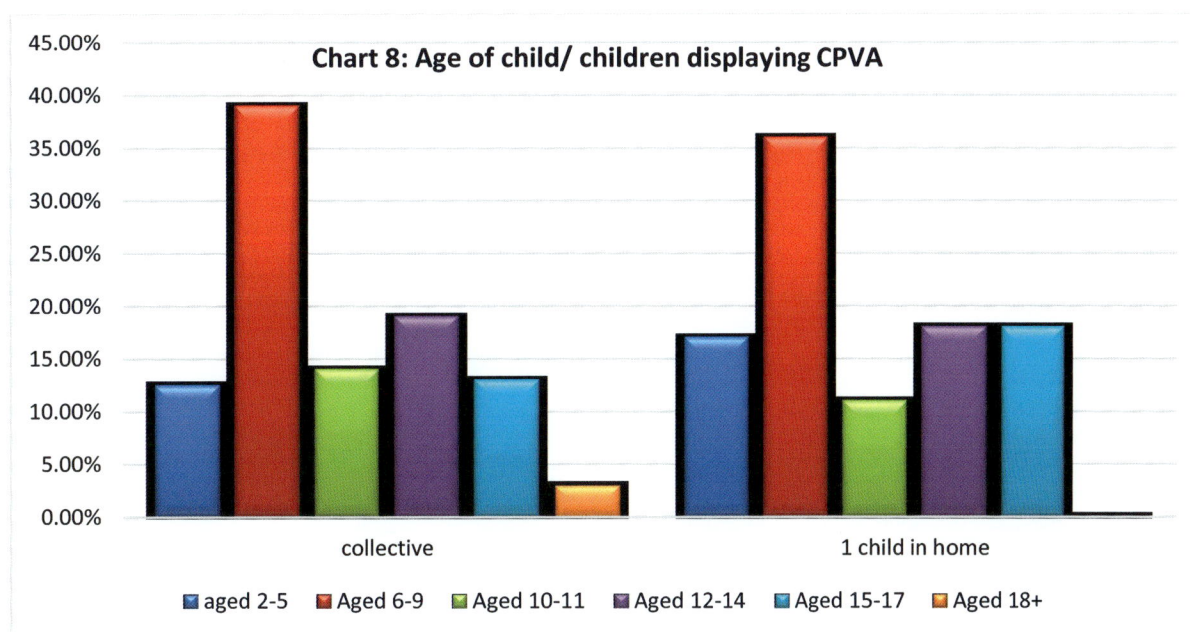

Chart 8: Age of child/ children displaying CPVA

Whilst Ullwin and Strauss pointed to the early years being the most prevalent time for CPVA, their results also reflected two specific age ranges where CPVA peaked before declining again. The first peak was seen at age 6 years (following a rise of 4% from age 5 years) then declining at age 7 years. The second peak was at aged 9 years (increasing by 5% from aged 8 years) before a decline by 5% at age 10 years. The findings outlined in Chart 8 support this position, in that the majority of children engaging in CPVA are aged 11 years or under. More notably what is also evident is that there is a clear 'dip' at age 10-11 years, before increasing again during adolescence; however, the increase is not at the same level as it was prior to the 'dip' occurring. The findings from Parentline (2008) raised similar indicators pointing to only 29% of CPVA starting in Adolescence, in this way ascertaining that younger child CPVA should be recognised. Parentline (2008) highlighted that in their survey the onset of aggression commenced at:

- 13% from birth,
- 27% during toddlerhood,
- 10% commencing school and a further
- 21% in middle childhood.

Furthermore, Breman and McRea (2017) noted in their report of CPVA towards carers (Kinship Carers and Special Guardians) it was children of 5 years of age displaying CPVA that was markedly higher than any other onset age, for engaging in acts of CPVA while in care. This contrasts with evidence pointing to CPVA increasing in adolescence, for example Simmons *et al* (2018) found in their review that the literature points to CPVA as an adolescent concern going onto note *This is consistent with research on age and offending generally, as well as general aggression, which shows a similar adolescent peak and reduction over the remainder of the lifetime.* This inconsistency may explain why the Home Office (2015, p.3- 1.1) produced guidance that dealt only with adolescence and not all children; however, in doing so their guidance fails to address the real issue, by overlooking the majority of children engaging in CPVA are not part of this adolescent indicator.

Perceiving CPVA as an adolescent concern helps to explain why there is so little guidance for professionals or families when seeking support, in that the Home Office focuses exclusively on adolescence, therefore guidance for CPVA reflects this focus within the UK. Such indicators help explain why those living with CPVA may struggle to ask for support, or gain support, when concerns are initially raised. The difficulty of seeking support when CPVA commences relates to how CPVA is perceived in society overall and the notion of regrading positions of power, between parent and child, when involving younger children. If parent/carers are encouraged to accept behaviour as age-stage normative, then they are less likely to seek early intervention. Furthermore, if they do seek intervention there are no established policies or guidance at this time to provide support for children under the age of adolescence. Left unsupported these families then experience escalating CPVA occurrence into adolescence when help is available, nevertheless families may then refrain from seeking help for fear of 'criminalising' their child. Likewise, a sense of 'shame' may also prevent families speaking out and seeking help, or the potential consequences for any siblings in the home if they are viewed to be 'at risk', or feelings of inadequacy being reinforced by suggestions of 'poor parenting', or 'unrealistic expectations', as noted in Thorley and Coates (2017b and c) such beliefs can all be barriers to families living with CPVA requesting support for the family.

In addition to their survey, Parentline (2008) analysed 3128 long calls relating to physical aggression and 6549 long calls relating to verbal aggression. They noted that

- 26% of calls relating to physical aggression were concerning children under 9 years of age and
- 17% of calls relating to verbal aggression were concerning children under 9 years of age.

Given the age of CPVA onset reported to Parentline (2008), where over 50% of callers stated CPVA commenced prior to middle childhood (outlined on page 35 of this report) compared to the age indicated at the point of making a 'long call' (as shown above), suggests that parents do not seek support as soon as they become concerned. Following the difference between when CPVA commences, to when parents contact Parentline (*ibid*), suggests that parent/ carers seem to wait until such time that they struggle to cope before making a long call; a suggestion that is also evident in the findings of Selwyn *et al* (2014) when discussing adoption breakdown. What is clear, throughout the literature to date, is the escalating nature of CPVA over time (as discussed in Adfam, 2012 and Selwyn, 2014 for example) and the potential for younger siblings to 'copy' CPVA behaviours, that in turn may help explain why sibling groups engage in CPVA, or some siblings within the home but not all children within the home. A further explanation of why CPVA may be displayed by one child but not another child, within the same family environment, at an earlier age than adolescence, may relate to those children with SEND. Some children with SEND who engage in CPVA may do so as a consequence of their diagnosis, if this is a condition that impacts upon their behaviour and emotional responses. In this way, those children with SEND may be the only child displaying CPVA within the household, irrespective of how many siblings are also resident within the home. Following this position, it can also be suggested that if children individually, or collectively as siblings, are engaging with CPVA as a consequence of their Adverse Childhood Experiences, it is then feasible that sibling CPVA may occur (due to the shared previous adverse experience these children may have had), reflective of what Van der Kolk (1994) proposed. Van Der Kolk argued that where emotional development continues to inform behaviour, even after children are moved to a safe environment, such behaviour can be directed at Adopters or Kinship or Foster Carers or Special Guardians. Nowakowski-Sims and Rowe (2017) go onto explain that this 'reactive' response has a direct correlation to any sense of helplessness the child felt previously during their childhood to date recognising Siegel's (2013) theory *that family violence is an outcome of emotional dysregulation created by exposure to traumatic stress, where such problems with emotional regulation are perpetuated from one generation to the next.* In this way where sibling 'groups' are placed together, following their removal from their home environment, these siblings may have experienced the same 'traumatic stress' and may have the same 'emotional dysregulation'. Alternatively, where a child alone is placed with other children in an existing household, they may struggle to manage their emotions towards these new siblings.

It is evident from the responses received that sibling CPVA is of concern, not only to the parent/ carers trying to manage more than one child who is engaging in CPVA, but the real risk these siblings may pose to each other, or any other siblings in the household. What is notable within the 2018 CPVA survey responses, is the number of families who are experiencing CPVA from one child within a multiple-child family. Within responses received 65% of participants were multiple-child families, as follows:

- 39% had two children,
- 23% had three children,
- 2% had four children and
- 1% had five children.

Across all of these multiple-child families it was predominantly one child that engaged in CPVA, so much so that in two child families 83% of these families lived with one child who engaged in CPVA, whilst the remaining 17% experienced CPVA from both children. A similar pattern was identified within three to five child families, whereby in three child families 77% lived with one child who engaged in CPVA (and thereby posing a risk to the remaining 2 siblings), 22.5% lived with two children engaging in CPVA and 0.5% experienced CPVA from all three children. However, when reflecting upon those families with four or five children, the majority of families experienced CPVA from one child and a small minority experienced CPVA from two children, but no family with 4-5 children experienced CPVA behaviour from more than two children overall. The age range indicator for multiple child families, where only one child engages in CPVA is similar to that of lone child families. These multiple child families also experienced CPVA behaviour predominantly during childhood, rather than adolescence, with a 'dip' at aged 10-11 years, before a further increase during 12-14 years of age. It was also interesting to note that within multiple-child families, where only one child engaged in CPVA, the predominant age for CPVA behaviour was at 6-9 years old, and accounted for:

- 64% of children in one child families
- 63% of children within two child families
- 73% of children within three child families

More markedly, when comparing those children aged 6-9 years to a collective adolescence age range (of 10-17 years), children aged 6-9 years remain the majority age range of children engaging in, or displaying, CPVA; whether they are the only child within the family, or one of multiple children, within the family. Similarly, children aged 6-9 years were prominent within data for multiple children displaying CPVA behaviour. Children aged 6-9 years accounted for one of the children in

- 80% of 2 child families where both children engaged in CPVA,
- 60% of families with 3 children (where more than one child displayed CPVA behaviour),
- 50% of families with 4 children (where more than one child displayed CPVA behaviour) and
- 50% of families with 5 children (where more than one child displayed CPVA behaviour).

In this way, children aged 6-9 years old appear to be included in the majority of homes where CPVA occurs, irrespective of whether any other children within the family. In this way, a child aged 6-9 years engaging in CPVA, were part of multiple child groups engaging in CPVA, that included children aged 2-5 years, 10-11 years, 12-14 years or 15-17 years. The age range of 6-9 years being predominant was also irrespective of whether there were two children, three children, four children or five children in the family overall. Such indicators highlight the necessity of reviewing CPVA guidance and support, to recognise adolescence may not be the age that guidance should be focused upon. Addressing the issue of CPVA occurring in families before adolescence is essential, not only for families but also for the children engaging in CPVA, if prevention of escalation or entrenched behaviour is to be addressed and prevented;

in order to provide restorative and effective interventions, that can reduce the risk of CPVA escalating during adolescence. Such findings support discussion and debate for recognising the challenges parent/ carers may encounter, when living with children that are Looked After, Previously Looked After or children with SEND, by acknowledging the distinctive difference between age-stage normative expectations compared to the behaviour noted by families to be of concern.

Analysis of responses, for the 2018 CPVA survey, highlighted that the majority of children aged 2-5 years displaying CPVA resided with siblings, across all multiple-child families groups. Such indicators underline the importance of listening to parents rather than attribute their concerns as over anxious parents, or as normative age-stage developmental expectations. Reducing behaviour displayed by children aged 2-5 years as age-stage normative expectations, rather than a concern by parents, reduces the behaviour to be a consequence of parenting capability or unrealistic expectations. In this way, such suggestions are dismissive of parents and will discourage parents seeking support in the future until the family reaches a crisis point. Following this argument, such discouragement then allows for behaviour traits displayed by older children to be 'copied' by this younger group. Moreover, in one response from a three-child family, CPVA is displayed by their 2-5 year-old, 12-14 year old and 15-17 year old, all of whom will require different interventions and strategies. Unfortunately, if as suggested previously, if these behaviour concerns are inappropriately identified as key age-stage development norms, such as toddler tantrums (aged 2-3 years of age), or adolescence hormonal adaptations (10-19 years of age), then these parents may be advised that it is they the parent/carer that requires support to parent effectively. This raises questions relating to what behaviours are anticipated, alongside who these behaviours are anticipated by,as part of developmental age-stage normative developments.

## What types of behaviour are displayed and how often?

Within the 2018 CPVA survey thirteen separate aspects of potential violent or aggressive behaviours were outlined, with the option to indicate as many as applied. These thirteen aspects of behaviour were repeated to enable different behaviour traits to be indicated for any sibling, within the same household, who was also engaging in CPVA behaviour. Within the options available five options reflected behaviours directed at the parent/ carer specifically, four options were focused towards any siblings and the remaining areas related to property damage or general threats. Overwhelmingly the most prominent CPVA behaviour displayed by the first (or only child), engaging in CPVA toward parents/carer, was that of physical violence or aggression without weapons, equating to 89% of responses. Alongside this, 81% of parents were also subjected to verbal threats that were aggressive towards the parent/ carer including shouting, swearing, name calling or threats of violence to provoke a reaction. The findings for verbal aggression resonate with previous findings over time, in that Parentline (2008) reported 60% of their 'long calls' related to verbal aggression. Verbal aggression is often sustained over a period of time and can be very loud causing parent/ carers significant distress, as a consequence of wording and emotional sentiment used. More recently Breman and MacRea (2017) reported that more than 80% of carers in their study had experienced 'psychological, emotional and verbal abuse', and Lee (2017) also highlighted similar findings.

The types of physical violence displayed without weapons includes kicking, biting, punching, slapping, grabbing, pushing or attempted strangulation, that for many parent/carer's resulted in bruising or physical injury, which previous studies have portrayed, are not so much individual incidents but sustained prolonged violent and aggressive periods of time. For more than 50% of those participating CPVA was experienced daily, this accounted for

- 28% of families in which CPVA occurred once or several times a day lasting less than an hour overall,
- 27% of families in which CPVA occurred once or several times a day lasting 1-3 hours overall and
- 6% of families in which CPVA occurred once or several times a day lasting more than 3 hours overall.

This means the majority of families living with CPVA do so on a daily basis (61%), highlighting the need for an urgent review of how CPVA is perceived, in terms of the impact on family life for everyone within the family household. At this time, in the UK, there are limited options available for families who are subjected to these daily behaviours, particularly if such behaviour is deemed to result from 'poor parenting'. To some extent the legal position does not help these families, should they seek support, in that if a child is placed on a Child Safety Order for example[17] in an effort to address the child's behaviour, the need for a Child Safety Order is perceived to be a consequence of parenting. Tees Safeguarding Children Board (n.d.) state that 'When a child is brought to the attention of the police or the wider community

---

[17] This places children under the supervision of the Youth Offending Team within England and Wales and can be used as a preventative intervention to reduce the risk of escalating behaviour that may be considered a criminal offence once the child is over 10 years of age as part of the Crime and Disorder Act 1998.

*because of their behaviour,* **this may be an indication of vulnerability, poor supervision or neglect in its wider sense**' (my emphasis); that by default may encourage the perception 'poor parenting' is a root cause of the behaviour displayed, should the parent/ carer seek support from the Police or another Authority representative. Conversely a Child Safety Order could be helpful if Local Authorities move beyond seeing this as a means of addressing 'poor parenting' to one that reflects 'supportive parenting', given Tees Safeguarding Children Board's Procedures (n.d.) also state that

> *The Child Safety Order (CSO) is a compulsory intervention available below the threshold of the child being at risk of significant harm. Children's social care can apply for a CSO where a child has committed an act that would have been an offence if s/he were aged 10 or above, <u>where it is necessary to prevent such an act, or where the child has caused harassment, distress or harm to others</u> (i.e. behaved anti-socially). <u>It is designed to help the child improve his or her behaviour,</u> and is likely to be used alongside work with the family and others to address any underlying problems.* (my emphasis)

In this way, a Child Safety Order may support families by default, in that once the Child Safety Order has been granted for the child the procedure should '<u>...offer them assistance and services that reflect their needs. This should be done on a multi-agency basis...</u> (my emphasis) (Tees Safeguarding Children Board). This means that the family could then receive support, assistance, interventions and where relevant training via a multi-agency network to help them manage their child's behaviour and reduce the risk of CPVA escalation; a position that the majority of families would welcome. To enable this to occur there is a need to move into a wider understanding of lack of parental control and recognise that 'lack of parental' control is not always by the choice of parent/ carers, nor the 'fault' of the parent; thereby recognising CPVA is not a behaviour that parent/ carers can 'control' without support, assistance and training where relevant. This is a pertinent point given the purpose of Child Safety Orders are a means of '*helping local authorities to positively intervene at an earlier stage in order to prevent the child's involvement in anti-social or criminal-type behaviour <u>from escalating into something more serious or becoming entrenched</u>*' (my emphasis) (Ministry of Justice, 2007). Taking into consideration the plethora of evidence that confirms, without intervention, pre-adolescence CPVA does escalate during adolescence and is often more violent and more aggressive, measures that intervene prior to this entrenchment or escalation are proactive, a step that may well prevent families seeking a Section 20 Care Order under the Children Act[18] (UK).

---

[18] Parent/ carers can request a Section 20 to be applied if the family home position becomes untenable, or siblings are at risk of harm from CPVA displayed within the home. Under Section 20 the LA has a duty to accommodate the

Alternatively, when the CPVA does escalate during adolescence, if it is more violent and more aggressive, the Police may charge the child once they are over the age of 10 years but remain under the age of 18 years[19]. This is an importance nuance if investigating ways in which to support families experiencing CPVA that may help reduce the risk of CPVA escalating into something more serious, or becoming entrenched, particularly for those families who do not experience CPVA on a daily basis at this time, but may do so in the future.

 In addition to those families who experience CPVA on a daily basis, 36% experience CPVA 2-3 times per week, 6% at least once per week, 5% experience 2-3 times a month and 3% once or twice per month. Moreover, 40% of families experience an increase in CPVA occurrences during holiday or celebration periods, such as birthdays or Christmas, highlighting how CPVA behaviours can and do 'escalate'. The potential for escalation, alongside the level and duration of physical 'assault' by children towards their parent/ carers is not unknown, for example Selwyn *et al* (2014, p.148) detailed *"She beat her dad up, she just started punching, and punching, kicking, and punching him, absolutely going berserk, I mean unhinged berserk…"* (p.148). Furthermore Boorman (2016) summarised her experience *"violence came out of the blue. Before you knew it an ordinary day could turn into one which may involve broken glass, chaos, blood, spit, vomit, urine and tears.."* whilst Mumdrah (2017) went further and summarised her experience that included

> *the bruises on my body that come, turn to rainbows, and then go.- the bite scars on my arms, and the deep raised one on my thigh- the regular scratch marks to my face, arms, back, legs, belly from the times I misjudge how close I can get to calm her while she tries to smash her head against the wall.- the burns from where she threw dinners or hot drinks over me.*

Adopter A (2017) outlined their personal experience to include:

> *For me, CPV is the worst part of adoption. It is the part that leaves me physically and psychologically battered and bruised. I am not a great physical healer, and after 4 months I have scars all the way up my arms from little fingernails and little teeth tearing at me like a wounded animal. I have bruises up and down my legs from kicks, and in my stomach from punches. I get almost PTSD-like symptoms when anybody*

---

child displaying CPVA whilst the parent/ carers retain all parental rights for the child. However, where this has been applied there are numerous posts within social media that point to parental rights being breached.

[19] If the child is under 10 years they cannot be charged with an offence, if aged 10-18 years they can be interviewed within police custody. If they admit to CPVA the child could then be given an informal caution, formal caution or be referred to the Family Court. If the child does not admit CPVA and the police proceed this will be considered in the Youth Court which could lead to a criminal record

*touches my hair suddenly, after a horrific prolonged and intentional attack when Wife had nipped out to run an errand one day.*

Whilst engaged in a sustained physical attack the majority of parent/ carers were also subjected to shouting and verbal aggression simultaneously, as Coates (2017) experienced

> *I'd consider it the most challenging experience of my life, day after day the assaults continued both physical and verbal. They had always been present in our family, low level name calling and hitting when frustrated or upset but then it got worse. It spiralled downward after a trip away, with normal routines gone for a single day a new pattern of behaviour emerged. Early the next morning it started. 'Stupid daddy'. Then fighting, hitting and biting. Rages that would last hour after hour with me standing between her and the rest of the family. I tried to hold her to keep her safe but that would prolong the rages but if I let go she'd come back to start again. We knew all the standard techniques, time out, appropriate consequences, carrots not sticks. She was four-years-old and I'd become afraid of her, nervous of when the next assault would come, I was covered in bites, scratches and bruises.*

In this way CPVA resonates with the behaviours associated with domestic abuse, albeit normally portrayed as adult to adult, but abusive none the less. Furthermore, many of these parents do experience actual physical harm that, if portrayed in any other context but the family home, could very well lead to prosecution given the age of criminal responsibility within England and Wales. This means all of those children engaging in CPVA over the age of 10 years, representing 46% of participant responses, could theoretically be held culpable for their behaviour, whilst those under 10 years could realistically be placed on a child safety order. Such possibilities deter parent/carers discussing CPVA outside of the home, particularly with Police or Social Work representatives, due to the nature of the longer-term impact on the child's life chances should prosecution ensue.  Moreover, where a sibling also engages in CPVA the attack on the parent/carer can become more sustained and abusive, particularly if siblings engage in CPVA simultaneously. Of those participating, in the 2018 CPVA survey, 20% of families (1:5 of those participating) experienced CPVA from more than one child within the family home. All parent/carers who experienced CPVA from 2 or 3 children were subjected to physical violence without a weapon by the second and third child. More concerningly 54% of parent/ carers living with one child that engaged in CPVA experienced physical violence with a weapon, that moves the potential for the 'abuse' to result in a more significant injury level. As noted by Hollins (2017) many such weapons used are those close to hand rather than pre-planned as such and include

- furniture (such as chairs, tables, lamps and so forth) to
- cutlery (including knives), tools (including chisels or screwdrivers) or

- crockery (including glass, plates and such like)

all of which contain the potential for 'occasioning actual bodily harm'[20]. Selwyn *et al* (2014p. 151) reported similar concerns *"We were surprised to find that 19 parents (27%), without prompting, reported worrying behaviour shown by their child around the use of knives. Parents described children who had used knives to threaten, intimidate, or control others."* In this way the urgency for recognising and addressing CPVA, within support services as a Multi-Agency approach is defined, without such discussion these children engaging in CPVA may go onto become part of the Youth Justice system, or as Selwyn *et al* reported, returned to Local Authority care via Section 20; either way it is far more cost effective to provide intervention prior to escalation than provide reactive measures following escalation.

Combined with physical violence (with or without weapons) 87% of parent/ carers were also subjected to verbal threats that were aggressive towards them in order to provoke a reaction; this included shouting, swearing, name calling or threats of violence, self-harm and suicide. In addition, 64% of families with one child who engaged in CPVA experienced emotional manipulation, where the child used emotional 'blackmail' to try to manipulate the parent/ carer into following their requirement. Some parents may go along with these requests in order to prevent escalation occurring that may lead to physical CPVA. This was also evident within families where more than one child engaged in CPVA, whereby 72% of families experienced emotional manipulation from the second child and 90% of families experienced emotional manipulation from the third child, who engaged in CPVA behaviours. With reference to threats of reporting the parent/ carer to authority figures,

- 32% of families with one child engaged in CPVA,
- 27% of families where two children engaged in CPVA and
- 50% of families where three children engaged in CPVA

adopted this approach as part of their CPVA behaviour. Within the UK, if children indicate to any authority figure (such as Teachers, Social Workers or Police) that they are being, or have been, threatened with abuse of any kind the 'authority' figure has a duty of care to instigate child protection processes and investigate the claims made. This can have a devastating impact on families, as noted within Thorley and Coates (2017b). Therefore, such threats made

---

[20] Occasioning actual bodily harm is a criminal offence within England and Wales and as such under UK Law can lead to prosecution and placing into a secure Young Offenders Unit.

to parent/ carers have to be viewed seriously, as some parents have found themselves in the midst of child abuse/ child protection investigations due to allegations made about them, from children displaying CPVA. For some parents such investigation can have a negative impact on their current or future employment, as well as resulting in them having to move out of the family home, or have children removed until the investigation is completed and, in this way, creating further Adverse Childhood Experiences for any other siblings within the family unit.

If viewing the impact of CPVA on siblings within the family then the potential for a Child Safety Order, as a means of addressing the impact for siblings living with CPVA, can be proactive tool; in that these children could be deemed to be at risk of harm from their violent or abusive sibling and are at the very least witnessing violence and aggressive behaviour within the family home, which by default is a form of domestic violence. Hollins (2017) pointed to 90.5% of CPVA displayed was violence or aggression towards others and pointed to *'Pushing sibling down the stairs'*, *'holding young sisters head under water in the bath'* and *'Slammed the car door on another child's hand on purpose...'* within behaviours involving siblings to provoke a reaction from the parent/ carer. Thorley and Coates (2017b and c) highlighted concerns about siblings was significant for parent/ carers, whilst Selwyn *et al* (2014) noted this as a main reason for placing those children displaying CPVA in Local Authority Care. The risk and harm to siblings from the child engaging in CPVA appears to be reflective of that to the parent/ carer themselves. Reponses indicated that in families where one child engaged in CPVA

- 51% experienced physical violence towards siblings (beyond the norm anticipated between siblings) without a weapon and

- 47% experienced verbal aggression towards siblings beyond the norm anticipated to provoke a reaction from the parent/carer.

This means that CPVA is not always directed towards the parent/ carer exclusively and children engaging in CPVA can focus their behaviour towards siblings, in order to generate a reaction from the parent/ carer. More concerningly, within 29% of families, where one child engaged in CPVA, physical violence was used towards a sibling that included the use of a weapon, which can cause actual bodily harm in much the same way this can when used towards the parent/ carer. Lastly, 29% of children displaying CPVA also used emotional manipulation of a sibling (beyond the norm), causing further distress to that sibling, as illustrated in chart 9.

## Chart 9: CPVA behaviour displayed towards siblings

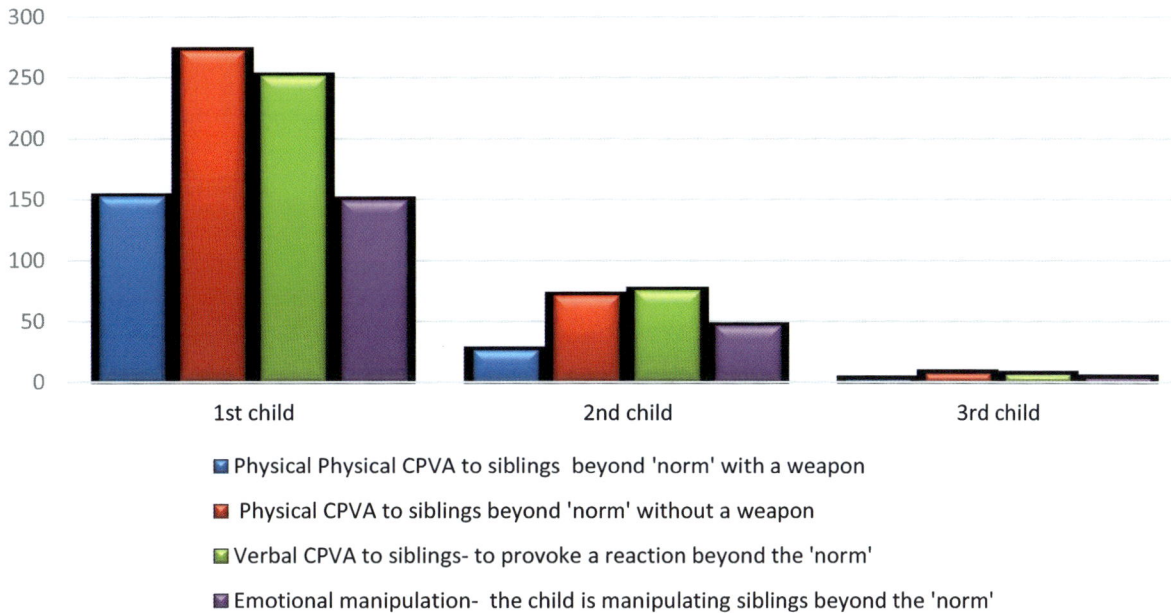

Legend:
- Physical Physical CPVA to siblings beyond 'norm' with a weapon
- Physical CPVA to siblings beyond 'norm' without a weapon
- Verbal CPVA to siblings- to provoke a reaction beyond the 'norm'
- Emotional manipulation- the child is manipulating siblings beyond the 'norm'

In multiple child families the indicators of CPVA involving siblings was similar to that found for CPVA involving parent/ carers; in that the majority of CPVA displayed by the second and third child, with reference to siblings, was physical violence without a weapon or verbal aggression. However, what this highlight's is the vulnerable position of those siblings, who do not engage in CPVA but reside in a family unit where CPVA occurs. They are in the same vulnerable position as any other child living with 'domestic abuse' and as such should be afforded the same service support as any other child at risk. This highlights the real problem of the current use for a Child Safety Order in supporting the family. Whilst a Child Safety Order can help support families by providing a pro-active multi-agency response to CPVA behaviour, including interventions to reduce occurrence and frequency, the original Crime and Disorder Act 1998 (part 3) states that 'the child has acted in a manner that caused or was likely to cause harassment, alarm or distress to one or more persons **not of the same household as himself'**. For this reason, the current terms of use for Child Safety Orders prevents these being adopted proactively to protect parents, carers or siblings within the same home environment; and in this way overlooks the consequences of CPVA completely when displayed by children under the age of 10. In overlooking the consequences to siblings living with CPVA (was well as adults within the family home), as well as failing to address the needs of the child under the age of 10 years engaging in CPVA, leaves siblings, parent/carer's and the child involved in CPVA, without real support until they reach the age where Police intervention can be provided[21]. In this way many of these children under the age of 10 years do not have their needs addressed, until such time they become a high risk of being part of the Youth Justice system (as they enter adolescence), that enables the Home Office (2015) directive for Adolescence to Parent Violence to be implemented. Waiting until the child reaches adolescence is not helping the child with their behaviour and promotes opportunities for the behaviour *'escalating into something more serious'* and become *'entrenched'* (Ministry of Justice, 2007); the opposite of what Child Safety Orders are supposed to provide. The only legal option then available to parent/ carers is to request a Section 20 for the child engaging in CPVA behaviour, that leads to the child being removed from the family home and accommodated by the Local Authority. If the CPVA displayed is consequential to early life experiences (ACEs), for example for those children who are Looked After, or have been Previously Looked After, applying a Section 20, leading to the removal of the child from the family home, could escalate the behaviour more readily as a further Adverse Childhood Experience. Should CPVA continue to be viewed as a legal argument (for when the child is older, such as that proposed by the Home Office, 2015) then the need for rethinking how Child Safety Orders are implemented is highlighted, in that the Child Safety Order would need to reflect the position of those families living with CPVA and be amended to protect and support families; through amending the Crime and Disorder Act 1998 (part 3) *'the child has acted in a manner that caused or was likely to cause harassment, alarm or distress to one or more persons* ==**either within or outside**== *of the same household as himself'* (amended wording highlighted with the removal of 'not' )

In addition to violence and aggression aimed towards the parent/carer or siblings, children engaging in CPVA can be destructive of property, either within the home itself, or of the home or vehicles belonging to the family. This is clearly seen in the reflections of Mumdrah (2017)

> *One hypothetical reference to collateral damage, that over the last 11 years has become a reality of:- an eight foot stretch of 150 year old T&G wood paneling now split, splintered and bowed out; her all time favourite self harm kicking place...six doors that no longer hang right, or close properly, and one with kick holes all across the bottom at different levels that represent the passing years like a height chart...- the 'road map' of our walls, criss crossed with skid marks from things hurled and whipped against them, - the oak kitchen table that survived our family for three generations, scarred with dozens of deep, double pointed dents from a claw hammer attack...- the long series of phones,*

---

[21] As previously noted If the child is under 10 years they cannot be charged with an offence, if aged 10-18 years they can be interviewed within police custody. If they admit to CPVA the child could then be given an informal caution, formal caution or be referred to the Family Court. If the child does not admit CPVA and the police proceed this will be considered in the Youth Court which could lead to a criminal record

*laptops, controllers, a hairdryer and a tv, all smashed to smithereens. With implements, and sometimes with her bare hands or feet; stamping or smacking them repeatedly until cuts bleed from the sharp edges…..- the dashboard of my land rover cracked and hanging off on the passenger side from full power kicks over the flavor of a packet of crisps…- the two lonely bowls left intact from a full dinner set, and the cracks in the tiles where the missing ones landed…- the banisters that creak and wobble a third of the way down where I crashed into them when she pushed me down the stairs…- the blinds from her room currently 'hidden' in a bin bag; stashed in the airing cupboard where she thinks I won't notice, cut into pieces…*

Hollins (2017) reported similar findings as did Breman and MacRea (2017), who noted this was substantive for Kinship Carers. In their report Breman and MacRea (2017) highlighted that nearly 40% of their participants reported behaviour that included 'hit or kicked a wall, door or furniture' and the majority was indicated as 'severe', echoing the notes made by Mumdrah (2017) of her experiences with reference to property damage. Furthermore, Beman and MacRea (2017) also noted that for 30% of their Carers the child had destroyed something belonging to them, whilst just over 30% had experienced threats to destroy their property. This highlights how the emotional impact may not be exclusive to name calling, verbal aggression or verbal threats but can also include the emotional impact of property destruction, theft of property, lying and/or stealing items from the home. Of those participating in this 2018 CPVA survey

- 78% of families where one child (or the first of multiple children),
- 72% of families where a second child displayed CPVA and
- 67% of families where a third child displayed CPVA

experienced damage to property and home items, including the child's own items. It is important to recognise this aspect of CPVA occurrence, given the current economic position within society today and the cost of repair or replacement for these damaged items, that for some families can become prohibitive. Such costs become more so where children displaying CPVA also engage in 'stealing' from the home (including money or items of reasonable monetary value), as indicated by Mumdrah (2017) "- *my christening bracelet, a part of me for 40 years, gone forever, without a trace"*. The sentimental value of such items, alongside the monetary value, increases the emotional distress experienced by these family units. A further aspect of CPVA displayed by children towards their family, similar to sibling threats, are threats towards someone outside of the home such as friends, teachers, relatives or family pets, again Mumdrah (2017) reflects "- *the canine tooth missing from my beautiful dog's mouth, broken by the rock hurled at her during an angry summer's day walk"*. Such action can increase the isolation of many families, who feel their situation is too volatile to risk travelling far from home. Hollins noted similar behaviour outside of the home stating

> *... There was a sense that violence could happen 'any time, any place, anywhere' ...Respondents revealed that incidents occurred 'on (the) pavement next to road', 'in A&E', on a 'hospital ward' and at 'school'. It is worth noting that several parents reported incidents taking place in the car; 'Trying to break the car glass window with head..', ... and 'Opening a moving car door on a fast road..'.*

This can then lead to family isolation and limited opportunities to engage in 'society' overall for fear of CPVA occurring. Concern over potential behaviours displayed outside of the home was indicated by more than 50% of respondents based on their experience of living with CPVA, irrespective of whether this was one child, two children or three children engaging in CPVA.

**Section Summary:**

This section highlights the complex multi-faceted nature of CPVA behaviours and the real risk these children, who engage in CPVA, pose to not only the parent/ carer but also to siblings. This section argues that a redrafting of the currently existing Child Safety Order, outlined within the Crime and Disorder Act (1998) could provide the support families request and require. Whilst it is recognised that this Order places the child under the supervision of the Youth Offending Team in England and Wales, the potential for rethinking its application is noted. The Child Safety Order is designed to provide multi-agency supportive interventions, as a proactive approach to reducing the risk of children, under the age of 10, behaving in such a way, that once they are over the age of 10 (the age of criminality within England and Wales) could result in criminal prosecution. Due to the existence of Home Office Guidance for Adolescent to Parent Violence, those children under the age of 10 years are overlooked. Applying the legal position, this means that these children engaging in CPVA tend to also be overlooked for support and do not receive sufficient timely intervention. Whilst the Child Support Order would not leave a 'criminal' footprint on the child's details, for when they are older and seeking employment, charges made after age 10 years might and result in limiting life opportunities for these children. The Child Safety Order in effect could help reduce this risk and support these children at the point of need, rather than waiting until they move into the criminal justice system for their CPVA behaviours. The restriction in using the Child Safety Order is based upon the wording used for application, in that this cannot be used if the behaviour is within the home environment, as such these can only be applied if the same behaviour is displayed outside of the home environment. If CPVA remains within a legal position, to be managed by the Police and Legal system, then having no safeguard in place prior to the age of 10 overlooks the risks posed to siblings as well as parents, carers or any other adult within the home environment. Such limitations also allow for the behaviour not only to escalate as the child moves into adolescence but also to become entrenched. The purpose of Child Safety Order is to address behaviours as a proactive early intervention, towards the prevention of the behaviour escalating or becoming entrenched, in this way the purpose of a Child Safety Order reflects the needs of families living with CPVA when viewed from a Legal position; whilst simultaneously being unavailable for families living with CPVA. Finally, what is clearly evident, is that children do not wait until adolescence to display or engage in CPVA and the indicative age for CPVA behaviours remains under 10 years of age. This in itself highlights the necessity to rethink current policies, that continue to argue CPVA is an adolescent concern, as a fundamental flaw in providing effective proactive support for families who experience CPVA within their home. If seeking to support families via the Child Safety Order this can be achieved by amending the Crime and Disorder Act 1998 (part 3) as follows *'the child has acted in a manner that caused or was likely to cause harassment, alarm or distress to one or more persons **either within or outside** of the same household as himself'* . the amendment *'not of the same household as himself'* to become 'either within or outside of the same household as himself'.

# 4. Let's Talk About:

# What causes children to behave this way?

Within the literature there has been a range of suggestions into the 'causes' of CPVA occurrence, including parenting approaches, neurological disorders and mental health indicators, all pointing to an increased risk for specific categories of children and young people. Current developments, by a number of leading practitioners, highlight the impact of loss and trauma on brain development, that then impacts on future learning, not solely as a consequence of neuron pruning in the early stages of development[22]. These indicators demonstrate why children and young people may function in their daily lives from a heightened state of 'alert', that in turn informs their behaviour and reactions (see for example NMT by Dr Bruce Perry and debate around Neurological development in the early years[23]). Alongside this a number of mental health and behaviour disorders listed within DSM-V[24] (or those noted within ICD-10/11) have been signposted as increasing the risk of CPVA, for example, existing studies linking ADHD to higher risk of engagement of CPVA behaviours. On the basis of this knowledge and understanding, it would seem apparent that parent/ carers need to be equipped from the outset to manage potential CPVA behaviours should this occur. This is not stating that CPVA *'will occur'* but recognises that it *'might* occur', as a co-morbid behaviour difficulty for these children. Therefore, it would seem prudent that those living within the same family are aware of this risk and can access the information, support and skills to support their child should this occur. Such provision, if it becomes necessary, should reflect a multi-agency approach and in this way, within the UK, would be addressed within an Educational Health Care Plan (EHCP) as a diagnosed behaviour condition in its own right.

The purpose of the EHCP is to recognise the child and the family require support to manage not only CPVA behaviour but also to limit the risk of such behaviour escalating or

---

[22] See for example publications and videos provided by Perry B .D., (The ChildTrauma Academy). (2013) 1: The Human Brain [Video webcast]. In *Seven Slide Series*. and Sarah-Jayne Blakemore (2012) the Mysterious Workings of the Teenage Brain

[23] Such as those identified by Perry and the ACE studies: The Adverse Childhood Experiences Study (**ACE Study**) Kaiser Permanente and the Centers for Disease Control and Prevention (1995-1997)

[24] DSM-V is the Diagnostic and Statistical Manual of Mental Disorders whilst ICD10 is the International Statistical Classification of Diseases and Related Health Problems- Mental Health and Behaviour Disorders are listed under category V

becoming entrenched. Unfortunately, the current processes for gaining support for children who engage in CPVA creates an impasse for many parents. This is due to how the current support systems are provided, in that to gain an Educational Health and Care Plan a child or young person needs to be struggling in their academic endeavours compared to their peers. Many families living with CPVA indicate that in reality the child is able to maintain their academic achievement to a sufficient level for the school purposes; therefore, they and their child are not eligible for EHCP support or resource provision[25]. Furthermore, within definitions of Special Educational Needs and Disabilities (SEND) used within the UK, under current legal statutes, there is little recognition of the 'disabling' impact mental and behaviour conditions can have for children and young people. This is highlighted for example if considering Post-Traumatic Stress Disorder (PTSD) or attachment difficulties. It would seem that this oversight fails to recognise the neurological impact on the brain specifically, in that there is now clear evidence PTSD for children is equal to that for veterans as shown in *'The PTSD brains of children and soldiers'* (McCrory 2016). The consequences for families by this oversight is highlighted within the findings generated for the 2018 CPVA survey, whereby all participants indicated a Health or Care need, if not an Educational Need, for the child or children that engaged in CPVA, many of who were without an EHCP.

Within participant responses almost 2/3rds of families had engaged in long assessment processes to be provided with an EHCP for their child. Such processes often commenced early in the child's formal education provision but did not complete until several years later. Unfortunately, this delayed period led to these families experiencing an escalation in the CPVA behaviour and witnessed the CPVA behaviour becoming entrenched. Of greater note is those families unable to secure the support at any time and were not in the process of receiving this support. For those families where only one child displayed CPVA, over 1/3rd had no support or planned support for the child or the family from any of the multi-agency services. In addition, where parent/carers had been declined an EHCP for their child, the majority of reasons provided were that the child 'managed' in school or could manage with low level support. Whilst this may be the case for some of these children, who engage in CPVA behaviours, if the EHCP is only provided for children 'struggling' in school then by default the priority is not so much the child holistically but

---

[25] For further detail of EHCP and definition of Special Educational Needs and Disability used within England and Wales refer to Appendix 1

the child academically. Following this position such argument views the child as an educational output rather than as a member of a family or as a member of society. This is important, in that all participants within the 2018 CPVA survey agreed that their child or children, engaging in CPVA behaviours, required additional support, if not at school then certainly outside of school. Such support was essential for the child or children to participate socially outside of the home as well as managing within the home. It can therefore be argued that whilst the current system points to supporting children with *'Educational, Health or Care'* needs this support system is a misnomer and fails to recognise those children with *'Care'* needs but not *'Education'* needs. This fundamental oversight neglects to acknowledge that some children may manage within formal education settings and conform to behaviour requirements but experience a build-up of emotional difficulty that is then displayed as CPVA when at home. This means parent/ carers who support children experiencing emotional regulation difficulty, displayed as violent, challenging or aggressive behaviour, are unable to gain support if such behaviour is not displayed within the formal school setting.

As a consequence of focusing exclusively on formal school interactions, the current system fails to distinguish where most children spend the majority of their time. The indicators generated within the data from the 2018 CPVA survey point to children and young people who struggle to regulate their emotions, or communicate difficulties they are experiencing, in any other way except via their behaviour. Given these children who engage in CPVA behaviour spend the majority of their time outside of the formal education setting, it would be pragmatic to include such difficulties in any assessment for support, to enable the child or children to participate within society alongside their peers. When children feel excluded as an outcome of their behaviour, or their mental or behaviour disorder, then their life chances can become limited, particularly if they:

- struggle to make, maintain and establish friendship groups
- lack the support they need to manage and 'cope' in society activities
- struggle with a sense of identity (often informed by peer networks)
- feel 'excluded' or as if they 'don't fit in'

The lack of multi-agency support provided for, through an EHCP, was also evident where a second or third child engaged in CPVA. Of those families with two children displaying CPVA behaviour 52% were without an EHCP and for families with three children displaying CPVA 58% were without an EHCP. Emerging within the data was the number of children diagnosed with behaviour or emotional difficulties, that are synonymous of SEND, for those children engaging in CPVA behaviour, as detailed within chart 10:

## Chart 10: CPVA and SEND

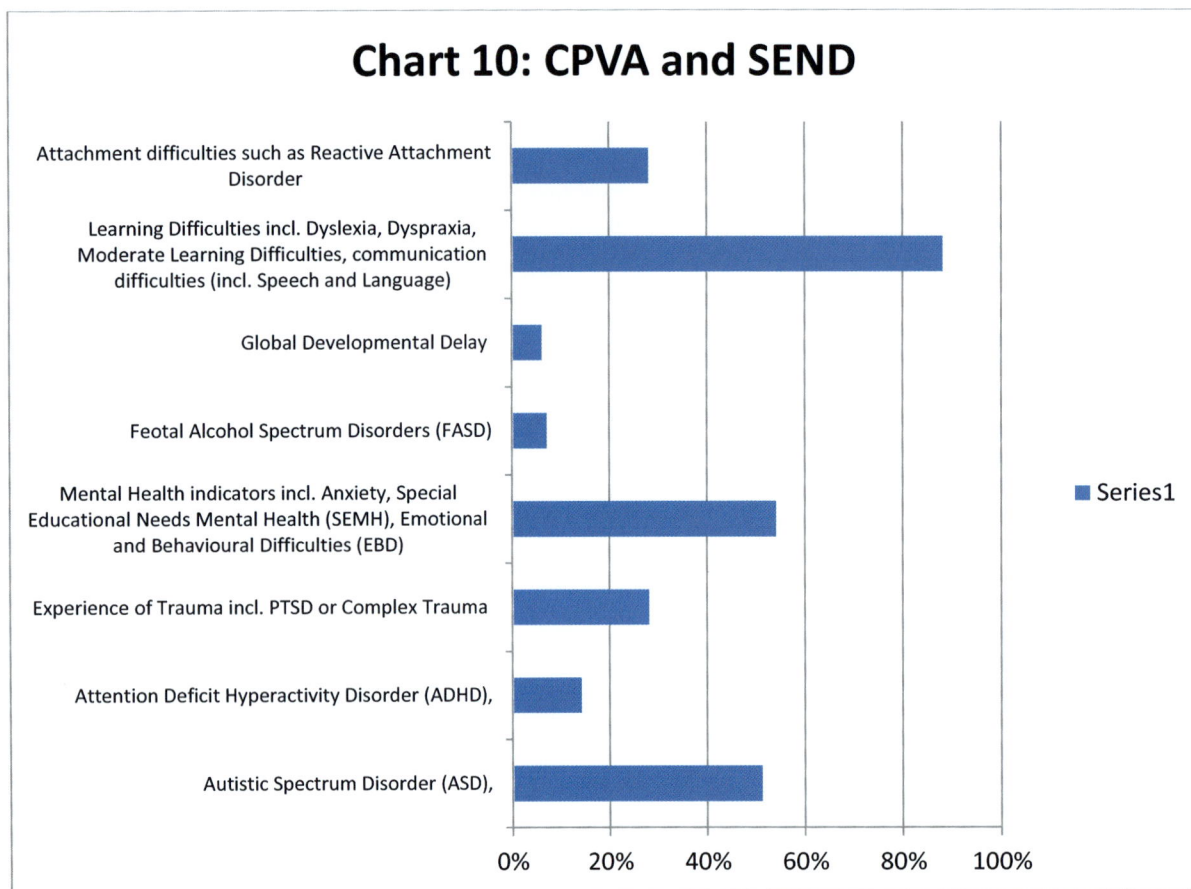

The need to recognise the impact of Neuropsychological/ Neurodevelopmental indicators, as a contributor of CPVA behaviours being displayed, is supported within participant responses; whereby more than 50% of participants indicated the child displaying CPVA had been diagnosed with 'Autistic and Learning Difficulties' and in this way pointing to why CPVA may occur. It is not unknown that children and young people with Autistic Spectrum Disorder or Learning Difficulties (or both indicators) struggle to communicate socially as a consequence of their diagnosed condition. This is clearly highlighted for families living with CPVA, whereby the participants pointed to a range of co-morbid emotional needs that included behaviour and communication difficulties, as detailed within chart 10. For families participating within the survey it was the dual diagnosis of 'Autistic and Learning Difficulties' that was most prevalent. However, the majority of families pointed to three co-morbid conditions alongside Learning Difficulties that included Attachment, Anxiety, Foetal Alcohol Disorders or Mental Health indicators such as anxiety and depression, that is highlighted by the volume of responses across the range of conditions noted. Anxiety and depression in relation to CPVA occurrence have been suggested in previous studies (Paulson et al. 1990; Calvete et al., 2012; Ibabe and Jaureguizar, 2012, Ibabe et al 2014b and 2014c). More specifically Kennedy et al (2010) recognised that in the United States, where adolescents had been charged with CPVA, there was a significant increase in suicide attempts and psychological stress of those charged. What was not as clear within studies (where anxiety or depression were noted as increasing the risk of CPVA occurrence) was the root cause of the anxiety or depression.

Confusion arises when CPVA is discussed as an element of a child's behaviour, that is overshadowed by the focus condition the child is being assessed for, as noted by Coogan (2014), who highlighted that whilst many children and young people were initially referred to CAMHS for Attention Deficit Hyperactivity Disorder or emotional and mental wellbeing (such as anxiety or depression) or challenging/ difficult behaviour; it was only after the initial consultation any discussion included CPVA. The problem of masking CPVA as a behaviour concern that may reflect a conduct disorder, on its own, arises when initial diagnosis is made; given that ICD-10 and ICD-11 (World Health Organisation, 2016 and 2018) includes 'Behavioural and emotional disorders with onset usually in childhood and adolescence (F90-F98); within which the descriptor outlines that the following applies:

> *Disorders characterized by a repetitive and persistent pattern of dissocial, aggressive, or defiant conduct. Such behaviour should amount to major violations of age-appropriate social expectations; it should therefore be more severe than ordinary childish mischief or adolescent rebelliousness and should imply an enduring pattern of behaviour (six months or longer**). Features of conduct disorder can also be symptomatic of other psychiatric conditions, in which case the underlying diagnosis should be preferred.**(my emphasis)

In this way the World Health Organisation descriptor may lead professionals to determine that children who display CPVA do so as a symptomatic behaviour of a different conduct disorder (such as Autism, Attention Deficit Hyperactivity Disorder, Post-Traumatic Stress disorder and so forth) rather than a Conduct Disorder in its own right. This approach reflects proposals by Coogan (2014) who noted that even when the issue of CPVA arose during assessment, this was noted as symptomatic of 'something else' rather than a concern on its own. It is for this reason that many parent/ carer's endure CPVA from younger children, believing their child's behaviour to be part of, rather than separate to, a behaviour concern or conduct disorder; for example: 'temper tantrums' rather than an indicator of CPVA or a 'settling in period' of 'challenging boundaries' for those who are Looked After or were Previously Looked After Children. Nonetheless, Breman and Macrae (2017, p.5) highlighted that becoming a child that is Looked After or having been Previously Looked After in itself is a traumatic experience for many children and is a transitional experience in which they have little or no say, due to the Court Order process determined by Adults. They argued that *"Just under half the carers reported experiencing family violence caused by the child in care. The majority of violence was caused by boys and younger children of both genders, suggesting trauma and distress emanating from children's experiences of trauma and separation from their parents"* (ibid p.5) a factor also indicated in previous studies[26]. What is highlighted within these studies is the relationship between mental wellbeing and the potential of CPVA occurrence. Ibabe *et al* (2013 p.527) concur with such suggestions and note that there is a clear correlation between CPVA and mental health, they continue and advocate that *"Serious mental illnesses, such as schizophrenia or bipolar disorders, seem infrequent in adolescents who abuse their parents. However, behavior disorders such as attention-deficit hyperactivity disorder, show special relevance"*. Whilst this suggestion could be seen to contradict the data generated by respondents within this 2018 CPVA survey, where 'Autism and Learning difficulties' is far more evident than ADHD, the data from this survey is restricted in its ability to generalise, due to how the survey was collected. Irrespective of this limitation it is evident that the relationship between those children diagnosed with behaviour disorders and CPVA occurrence is significant, yet this could to some extent be anticipated and expected. If reflecting on the 'Coventry Grid' (2015) indicators to differentiate between Autistic Spectrum Disorders and Attachment difficulties both point to difficulties with emotional regulation, that could lead to behaviour resonate with CPVA; of note, within Section 6.1, it is clear how children with Autistic Spectrum Disorders and children with Attachment difficulties struggle with emotional regulation as follows:

> *Typical Presentation in ASD-*
> *Extremes of emotion may provoke anxiety and repetitive questioning and behaviour…*
> *Does not easily learn management of emotions from modelling … Emotions take over*
> *from* **logic**/*knowledge of what one should do… Does not show displays of emotion to*
> *everyone …(e.g.never has a temper tantrum in school… Cognitive empathy is poor* (my
> extract and emphasis)

---

[26] see for example Cottrell, 2001, and more recently Coogan and Lauster, 2015; as well as Selwyn and Meakins, 2015; who similarly highlight this issue.

*Typical Presentation in Attachment Problems-*
*Difficulty coping with extremes of emotion and recovering from them (e.g. excitement,*
*fear, **anger**, sadness)…May provoke extreme emotional reactions in others …Shows*
*emotional displays to people child does not know (indiscriminate) and tends to carry on*
*longer (e.g. temper tantrums occur anywhere and at any time)…* (my extract and
emphasis)

This points to a range of specific conditions that present a higher risk of CPVA occurrence, yet

such potential and possibility is not explored within support provided; insomuch as families

discuss difficult behaviours as symptomatic of the condition rather than as a condition in itself,

in the same approach that professionals appear to adopt. Similar difficulties were noted by

Gallagher (2008) who noted that the focus for behaviour tended towards any medical

condition and if a condition could not be identified then such behaviour was perceived to fall

within one of the DSM-V areas such as Attention Deficit Hyperactivity Disorder. The

predicament created and questions raised for families, when adopting this stance, relates to

information provided at the point of diagnosis.  If CPVA is symptomatic of an underlying

condition, parents should be informed of this possibility, yet it appears that this does not

occur and leaves parent/ carer unprepared should this occur. Preparing families for possible

CPVA occurrence enables those parent/carers to undertake any training they may require, in

order to be skilled and effective should the child engage in CPVA. In this way equipping them

with the skills and knowledge to support the child, or children engaging in CPVA, enables them

to keep themselves, their child and any siblings in the home, safe from harm given the 'sudden

mood changes' these children can display. However, it also need to be noted that not all

children, with a conduct disorder that increases the risk of CPVA occurring, will actually engage

in CPVA. Parent/ carers need to be informed of the increased risk, around CPVA occurrence, as

a possible behaviour trait rather than a definitive behaviour trait and offered sufficient

resources to equip them in providing early intervention should this trait occur. More

importantly early intervention may de-escalate the situation and prevent the behaviour from

becoming established or entrenched. This is pertinent to those conditions where the risk of

CPVA occurring as a behaviour trait is high, for example as seen in Pathological Avoidance

Demand. The Pathological Avoidance Demand Society (UK) offer the following within their

handbook for Health, Education and Care practitioners:

*Most parents report having to handle their child with 'velvet gloves' and find themselves*
*constantly treading on eggshells. Mood is unstable with swings that are sudden and*
*dramatic. Changes of emotional state may be sparked by trivial issues, but frequently*
*occur without obvious triggers, apparently coming out of nowhere. Behaviours can*
*appear to be at the extreme end of 'the terrible twos' and parents may not be unduly*

*concerned until it is apparent that this is not merely a passing phase that they will grow out of. Getting a child to comply with the most basic day to day requirements of life is a challenge and the same battles are fought every day.* (my emphasis). Pathological Avoidance Demand Society (2016)

This clearly illustrates that there is a potential for CPVA occurring within the family at some point for **Pathological Avoidance Demand** but is not isolated to only **Pathological Avoidance Demand**. Studies conducted to date that have interrogated the relationship between CPVA and DSM-V classifications (American Psychiatric Association, 2013) point to *Disruptive, Impulse-control and Conduct Disorders* (Ibabe et al, 2014c) alongside Attention Deficit Hyperactivity Disorder, as increasing the risk of CPVA behaviours. This reflects previous findings by Anderson (2011) that involved 1,380 children with Autistic Spectrum Disorder, following which they pointed to 56% of their study group displaying CPVA and highlighting that:

> *"This new study provides confirmation that aggression is a major issue for caregivers of children on the autism spectrum, validating the experience of many and laying the groundwork for future research. It underscores the need for interventions to address aggression in children with ASD, and to support families coping with it"* (op.cit).

Such suggestions are supported within the findings of this 2018 CPVA survey data, where all of the conditions listed by participants for their child or children included behaviours that resonate with *Disruptive, Impulse-control and Conduct Disorders*[27]. More specifically 86% of families where one child displayed CPVA, 57% of families where two children displayed CPVA and 63% of families where three children displayed CPVA felt the behaviour was a reflection of previous 'trauma' and in this way a reactive emotionally dysregulated behaviour.

Emotional difficulty or dysregulation also exists when these children attend school, despite these families lacking an EHCP for SEND and despite the child who engages in CPVA demonstrating they are experiencing *'a significantly greater difficulty in learning than the majority of others of the same age'* as outlined within SEND principals. Whilst some children who engage in CPVA appear, at surface level, to manage within school many do not. Participant responses reflected 76% of children who engaged in CPVA had experienced a wide

---

[27] The American Psychiatric Publishing Textbook of Psychiatry , (6th Ed.) (2014) . Chapter 22. Indicates that within Disruptive, Impulse-Control, and Conduct Disorders *The common thread that runs through these disorders is an underlying construct of emotional and/or behavioral dysregulation that results in impulsive behavior, aggressiveness, and pathological rule breaking. ... they are classified within DSM-5 together with disorders of impulse control that typically persist into adulthood.* (Hales R. E, Yudofsky S. C, Weiss Roberts L) (eds)

range of sanctions within school as a result of their behaviour. This ranged from 1 in 3 children (occasionally) to 1 in 4 children (frequently) who lost merit points or had sanctions imposed, as a behaviour management approach. Another approach for managing behaviour difficulties displayed by pupils in schools was to move the child to an isolation area; this led to 16% of the children engaging in CPVA at home being moved to work in isolation frequently or occasionally, but certainly at some point. More concerningly 1:4 had been excluded from school as a consequence of their behaviour. What is not noted within the exclusion indicator, is that whilst this may resolve the issue of managing the child's behaviour in school, it increases the risk of escalating the incidence of CPVA for parent/ carers if the child is at home during school hours.  In addition to these excluded children, there are those children who engage in CPVA and are home-schooled. Of those participating in the 2018 CPVA survey, 1 in 4 children were not educated within mainstream provision as follows:

- No longer attends provision and is home schooled- 5%
- No longer attends provision and we are waiting for another provision/ suitable school- 7%
- Has never attended provision and has been home schooled as a family choice- 1%
- Has never attended provision and has been home schooled due to lack of suitable provision in my area- 1%
- Receives an alternative provision (including part-time provision. part-time home school) 12%

These indicators are not unknown for children with SEND, or for children who are Looked After, or have been Previously Looked After; in that current concerns relating to children's aggressive, abusive, violent or challenging behaviour has led to increasing numbers of children being excluded from school, yet there appears to be little support provided within the home by the 'excluding' Local Authority. More often than not parents report that it is they, the parent, that is required to change the behaviour displayed by their child, in order to ensure the child is able to conform to the educational placement expectations; for many parents this leaves them with little option but to undertake to educate their child at home. In addition to the education of the child at home, parent/carers are also then responsible for managing the child's behaviour, irrespective if this leads to an escalation in CPVA occurrence or results in the behaviour becoming entrenched.

For many parent's respite from the risk of CPVA occurrence is only gained whilst the child is in school, therefore any respite gained is negated if the child is excluded. Within responses for this survey only 1% opted to home school by choice, with the remaining 25% being placed into this position due to part-time provision, lack of choice in area or permanent exclusion that is unresolved.  This poses a range of issues that are not addressed through exclusion, not only for parent/ carers such as their employment opportunities and sense of own identity, but also for children who may already be struggling with emotional regulation.  Nowakowski-Sims and Rowe (2017) pointed to CPVA as a potential coping strategy that can be amplified when further adversity occurs. Such amplification results from a perception of self (such as being excluded and the loss of any friendship group or sense of belonging). For the excluded child their sense of value, worth, esteem and image may be negated and they can feel that they are 'less worthy' than their peers. Unfortunately, those children who are a Looked After or have been Previously Looked After, or a child with SEND, already hold self-negative views that being excluded reinforces. Such self-belief held by children can then reduce the child's ability to regulate or manage their emotions leading to an escalation of CPVA occurrence. This is predominantly relevant to those children who have a higher Adverse Childhood Experience (ACE) score.

Adverse Childhood Experiences are evident for increasing the risk of mental health and behaviour indicators in children, young people and adults. Nowakowski-Sims and Rowe (2017 p.266) agree that mental health indicators are significant, noting that *Childhood adversity places youth at risk for internalizing behaviors (i.e. anxiety and depression) and externalizing behaviors (i.e. aggression).* This suggests when seeking intervention and support for children who engage in CPVA, an assessment of Adverse Childhood Experiences should be included by qualified paediatric psychiatrist, psychologist or mental health specialist. This would enable the overall mental wellbeing of the child to be ascertained and clarify if internalised Adverse Childhood Experiences are informing current internalised or externalised behaviour, including CPVA (this should also include a full pre-natal account to exclude for example Foetal Alcohol Syndrome). The need for more comprehensive understanding of ACE's in the context of CPVA may provide insight into how and why a higher prevalence of CPVA occurs in, for example: adoptive, foster care, kinship care or Special Guardian families. Such correlation may also provide insight into any higher risks of CPVA behaviour displayed by those children diagnosed with Foetal Alcohol Spectrum Disorders, prior to the behaviour commencing. A further correlation may provide insight into Looked After Children or Previously looked After Children who display CPVA at a later age, rather than at age of placement, when reflecting upon their previous earlier life experiences; for example, it is well documented that

- Higher levels of ACEs lead to a higher risk of Alcohol or Drug misuse
- Alcohol or Drug misuse by adolescents leads to a higher risk of CPVA behaviour occurring

Nevertheless, there are few studies to date that have correlated ACE scores to alcohol or drug related CPVA specifically. Moreover, it is well documented that experiences and neurological brain patterning, developed pre-natal and during the early post-natal periods, predominate how the growing child thinks and behaves (see for example Perry, 2006). Such association is synonymous with Van der Kolk's (2014) concept in relation to adverse childhood experiences and 'The Body Keeps the Score' that provides insight into the why CPVA externalised behaviour may surface, particularly when this involves children who are Looked After or Previously Looked After; irrespective of the fact that these children have moved to a different family environment to that of their birth family where the adversity occurred. Van der Kolk recognised, that even when placed within a safe and secure family environment, the internalised feelings and sensations previously experienced continue to inform the child's mental wellbeing and consequently their externalised behaviour. This highlights the need to determine ACEs within any CPVA discussion, in order to acknowledge the longer-term impact of internal and external emotional regulation of those displaying CPVA, as an instrumental influence in their overall life outcomes. Previous studies have consistently reported poorer life outcomes for children who are Looked After, Previously Looked After and children with SEND, leading to a significantly higher proportion of these groups of children

- experiencing mental health difficulties,
- becoming part of the youth justice system,
- engaging in risk taking behaviours as well as
- underachieving academically.

Such argument then points to an increased risk of children who are Looked After, Previously Looked After and children with SEND being proportionally more likely to behave in ways that resonate with CPVA than their peers; by recognising that their SEND diagnosis, or their ACE score, may influence their emotional regulation and subsequently their mental wellbeing. There is significant support for Achenbach and Edelbrock (1978) in noting the presenting behaviour can be viewed as an accumulation of both internal and external manifestations; as suggested by Bonnick (2016) who reflects that *"The further I have looked at the issues the more I am drawn to the centrality of trauma for many of the young people across the board, whether in witnessing DV, experiencing CSE, being involved in gangs or criminal activity"*. This is an important point, particularly in the UK, given the recent Children's Commissioner report into vulnerable children across England (2017). The Children's Commissioner suggests as many as 460,000 children are involved in 'gang' activity and much of their activity within these 'gangs' was linked to drug mules or sexual exploitation with as many as 1,200 under 15-year olds engaged as 'modern slaves'. However, there is also a need to recognise that many children, particularly in adolescence, struggle to externalise their feelings through discussion and that this difficulty can then lead to externalised behaviour, including CPVA. For some children this can be as part of a diagnosed mental health condition that includes an impact upon cognitive functioning (Neuropsychological/ Neurodevelopmental) as an internalised indicator, for example:

- emotional and behavioural regulation,
- working memory ability,
- attention deficit,
- struggling to decode social cues,
- low self-esteem,
- social isolation,
- attention seeking,
- low self-confidence,
- poor self-image or notions of worthlessness.

Such internalised perceptions can then lead to externalised aggressive behaviour towards parents/ carers. Likewise, if expanded and analysed against the number of children who have been diagnosed with emotional or behavioural SEND specifically, that also display CPVA (for example Autistic Spectrum Disorders, Attention Deficit Hyperactivity Disorder, Reactive Attachment Disorder, Post Traumatic Stress Disorder), greater insight of how and why children, who are Looked After or were Previously Looked After, may engage in CPVA can be generated; despite these children moving to a different family environment to that of their birth family. Such indicators enable recognition that children who have a diagnosis such as Autistic Spectrum Disorder (ASD), Attention Deficit Hyperactivity Disorder (ADHD), Reactive Attachment Disorder (RAD) or Post Traumatic Stress Disorder (PTSD) may display CPVA, as symptomatic of their condition and in this way their CPVA behaviour is without 'intention'. Following this argument suggests that CPVA can be seen, for some children, as a behaviour that is a co-morbidity to their condition; when that condition includes difficulties in regulating their emotional responses particularly towards their parent/ carers. However, some studies have suggested the inability to regulate emotionally leading to CPVA behaviours are symptomatic of how the parent/ carer interacts with the child, rather than a conduct disorder in its own right, and results as an outcome of their parenting approach.

Emotional regulation and ability to regulate emotions is noted in much of the literature to date, as an indicator of CPVA, with associated discussion around parents who have unrealistic expectations, deficit communication skills, poor parent discipline/supervision or inability to provide appropriate emotional support (Kennedy et al, 2010; Calvete et al., 2012; Ibabe, 2014 and 2016). Such indicators correlate positive-parent relationships and experience as the intervention required, in so much as Ibabe (2016) points out that positive-parent relationships are considered as a 'protective factor' in CPVA. This raises issues for Foster Carers, Kinship carers, Special Guardians or Adopter family units, in that they may provide a positive-parent relationship built over time, but this does not erase early trauma experiences that inform child behaviours. Such behaviours can include CPVA as a behaviour developed from previous Adverse Childhood Experiences (see for example Nowakowski-Sims and Rowe, 2017). Moreover, whilst there is much discussion around parenting, including authoritarian and permissive parenting, this does not appear to account for those families who are parenting children who experienced early trauma or loss, such as those parenting a Looked After or Previously Looked After child or a child with SEND. At face value many of these parents (parenting a Looked After or Previously Looked After child or a child with SEND) do not reflect parents with unrealistic expectations that could lead to a higher incidence of CPVA, yet they still experience CPVA.

Employing parenting approaches as a potential indicator for CPVA occurrence that reflect those proposed by Baumrind (1966) as authoritarian, permissive and authoritative; or those that also include Maccoby and Martins (1983) neglectful parenting approach, are limited in the reality for parenting children who are a Looked After or Previously Looked After or have SEND. Maccoby and Martin (ibid) developed the approaches outlined by Baumrind and recategorised these as authoritative-reciprocal, authoritarian-power assertive, permissive-indulgent and permissive-indifferent, that have been applied to previous studies relating to CPVA-parenting correlates. Previous studies point to a higher risk of CPVA occurrence when parents are permissive or authoritarian[28] (for example: Pagini, 2004; Cottrell and Monk, 2004; Cottrell, 2005; Calvete et al, 2013; Margolin and Baucom, 2014; Hoskins, 2014; Ibabe, 2016, Kauy et al, 2017). However, within the literature to date is there is a clear omission of 'therapeutic parenting' approaches. This is significant if constructing any correlation between parenting and CPVA, in order to reduce any risk of 'therapeutic parenting' being misconstrued as permissive parenting. If therapeutic parenting is construed as permissive parenting then interventions become focused upon parenting behaviours, rather than child or adolescent behaviours. Furthermore, if focusing on the parent and their parenting approach all subsequent intervention, support and services then view the adult as problematic (as a result of their parenting) rather than recognising therapeutic parenting is the underpinning approach required. Therapeutic Parenting is advocated for the successful parenting of those children who have experienced significant loss or trauma or for a Looked After or Previously Looked After[29] child or a child with SEND. In this way, including and recognising 'therapeutic parenting' as proactive parenting becomes essential, when employing studies related to parenting and CPVA risk factors. Therefore, all future studies, investigating parenting and CPVA risk, require a re-construction of recognised parenting; to reflect five parenting approaches rather than the four noted by Maccoby and Martin. In addition to parenting approaches, emerging studies need to account for the wider indicators of children who have experienced loss or trauma, particularly for those children who have experienced significant loss or trauma or are Looked After or Previously Looked After[30] or have SEND; as it is recognised that these children are significantly more likely to engage in risk taking behaviours compared to their peers, irrespective of parenting, particularly as they enter adolescent. Such indicators are noted within a range of previous reports including for example Hanson and Holmes (2014) who pointed to adolescent behaviour as an adaptive response embedded within negative early life adversities or experiences that Nowakowski-Sims and Rowe (2017) as well as Simmons *et al* (2018) agreed was a significant contributor to CPVA[31]. In this way it is essential that any real engagement with CPVA addresses both the internal and external influences upon the child's behaviour and position these not only within their current family but any previous family/home environment they have experienced.

---

[28] It is suggested CPVA is particularly evident where physical punishment is used or aggressive verbal reprimands whilst Margolin and Baucom (2014) noted *mother to child aggression was the strongest indicator of physical CPV* whilst Hoya- Bilbao et al (2018) pointed to corporal punishment by parents associated with CPVA in adolescent Spanish Teenagers

[29] including children who are adopted, living with family members (Special Guardianship or Kinship).

[30] including children who are adopted, living with family members (Special Guardianship or Kinship).

[31] Nowakowski-Sims and Rowe (2017) and Simmons et al (2018) concur indicators within the previously published ACE study (1995-1997) were evident in higher risk of CPVA occurring

It is evident that whilst there have been a number of studies to date seeking to provide clearer understanding of CPVA, recognising CPVA as a co-morbid condition does not appear to have been studied in any great depth; rather it has been studied as a 'part' of something else. This creates real limitations in understanding, in that whilst there are correlations of risk noted within studies 'of something else' (such as Autistic Spectrum Disorders, Foetal Alcohol Syndrome, Attention Deficit Hyperactivity Disorder) not all children diagnosed with these behavioural conditions will display CPVA; in much the same way as not all children who are Looked After or have been Previously Looked After engage in CPVA. Recognising CPVA as a diagnosable condition, in its own right, is the first step to acknowledging the existence of CPVA and provide support for those living with CPVA. This is important in that there is a diagnosable condition within the DCM-V and ICD-11[32] indicators that recognises CPVA exists, yet to date no family living with CPVA has indicated their child has been assessed for this, let alone diagnosed. This is potentially the main oversight in discussing CPVA to date. Within Neurodevelopmental Disorders (World Health Organisation, 2016 and 2018) the diagnostic criteria emphasise a need to assess both 'adaptive functioning' and 'cognitive capacity'; however, there is an emphasis on determining the severity of Neurological conditions by 'adaptive functioning' rather than any IQ score (cognitive functioning); in doing so this would allow for the potential diagnosis, of a range of conditions, that the parent/ carers participating in the 2018 CPVA survey have stated apply to their child who engages in CPVA. Building on these Neurological conditions *(ibid.)* ICD-10/11- V includes 'Behavioural and emotional disorders with onset usually in childhood and adolescence' (World Health Organisation, 2016 and 2018; F90-F98); within which the descriptor outlines that the following applies:

> *Disorders characterized by a repetitive and persistent pattern of dissocial, aggressive, or defiant conduct. Such behaviour should amount to major violations of age-appropriate social expectations; it should therefore be more severe than ordinary childish mischief or adolescent rebelliousness and should imply an enduring pattern of behaviour (six months or longer). Features of conduct disorder can also be symptomatic of other psychiatric conditions, in which case the underlying diagnosis should be preferred.* (my emphasis)

This has potentially led to CPVA being associated as a behaviour trait within another condition rather than a co-morbid possibility, that recognises not all children with the 'other condition' display CPVA behaviour. Within the specifications for Conduct Disorder there are a range of

---

[32] ICD-11 World Health Organisation is currently updating the indicators and details of Behavioural Disorders and Neurological disorders to reflect new understanding in this area. The 11th edition of the International Classification of Diseases and Related Health Problems (ICD-11) is expected to be approved by the World Health Assembly in 2018

conditions pertinent to families living with CPVA, of note F91-0 (ICD-11) (World Health Organisation, 2018) is listed as a *Conduct disorder confined to family context* furthermore, for classification F.91 the World Health Organisation state this applies to:

> *Conduct disorder involving dissocial or aggressive behaviour (and not merely oppositional, defiant, disruptive behaviour), in which the abnormal behaviour is entirely, or almost entirely, confined to the home and to interactions with members of the nuclear family or immediate household.*

and in this way directly reflects the parent/carers responses of CPVA behaviours within the home, not only in the 2018 CPVA survey, but also those previously reported (including for example: Anderson, 2011; Calvete *et* al, 2012; Gordon and Wallace, 2015; Bonnick, 2016; Boorman, 2016; Adoption UK, 2017; Thorley and Coates, 2017). This suggests that whilst growing evidence highlights CPVA is a real concern, the potential for supporting families within Health perimeters has been available for some time but is yet to be applied. The basis for recognising CPVA as a Health concern, rather than a 'Policing' concern; resides in how CPVA is discussed. Viewing CPVA as a 'violent' or 'aggressive' behaviour that the child has intentionally engaged in, has led to the broader use of the term CPVA as a collective behaviour. In this way focusing exclusively on the behaviour displayed has resulted in all children to be seen to be intentionally engaging in CPVA. This has then led to the professional and societal response of countering parental/carer concerns as requiring a 'legal' intervention. Following on from this, having determined CPVA is intended and an 'illegal' reflection of domestic abuse points to the solution to be a 'Police' response. Whilst it is not proposed that all children who engage in CPVA should be diagnosed with the Conduct Disorder, outlined within the World Health Organisation ICD-10/ ICD-11 F91-0; neither should all children who engage in CPVA be viewed as doing so intentionally. It therefore appears evident that a new way of understanding is required, one in which there is recognition that some children will engage in CPVA with purpose and intent, as currently defined and outlined by Holt (2014); that reflects the minority of children displaying CPVA in the home. For the majority of children engaging in CPVA, this should be rephrased and described, discussed and researched as a *Conduct disorder confined to family context* (WHO, 2018) thereby eliminating any confusion between causes, risks and consequences. Alternatively, there is potential to place CPVA behaviours within ICD-10, F98-9 *'unspecified behavioural and emotional disorders with the onset usually occurring in childhood or adolescence'* given that this includes the following (*ibid*):

1. A classification of disorders in the diagnostic and statistical manual of mental disorders (dsm) that are usually diagnosed in *infancy, childhood or adolescence and are characterized by an individual's inability to behave in a cooperative manner*. (my emphasis)

2. A disorder diagnosed in childhood or adolescence age group *characterized by aggressive behavior, deceitfulness, destruction of property or violation of rules that is persistent and repetitive, and within a one year period*. (my emphasis)

3. A repetitive and persistent pattern of *behavior in which the basic rights of others or major age-appropriate societal norms or rules are violated. These behaviors include aggressive conduct that causes or threatens physical harm to other people or animals, nonaggressive conduct that causes property loss or damage, deceitfulness or theft, and serious violations of rules. The onset is before age 18*. (from dsm-iv, 1994) (my emphasis)

4. *Any of various conditions characterized by impairment of an individual's normal behavioral functioning, and caused by social, psychological,* biochemical, genetic, or other factors, such as infection or head trauma. (my emphasis)

5. Disorders characterized by persistent and repetitive patterns of behavior that violate societal norms or rules or that seriously impair a person's functioning. Compare behavior problems.

6. *Mental disorder of childhood and adolescence characterized by repetitive and persistent patterns of conduct in which rights of others and age-appropriate societal rules are violated; the conduct is more serious than ordinary mischief and pranks*. (my emphasis)

7. *Repetitive and persistent aggressive or nonaggressive behavior in which basic rights of others or social norms are violated*. Self esteem is generally low, and an inability to develop social relationships and lack of concern for others may or may not be present. (my emphasis)

In addition to the criteria outlined within the World Health Organisation ICD-10/ ICD-11, the DSM-V manual (American Psychiatric Association, 2013) outline the criteria for Conduct Disorders; they stipulate that to be diagnosed the child must display at least three out of fifteen symptoms within the previous 12-month period, in addition one of the symptoms must be displayed within the previous six months. These symptoms are outlined in Table 1 (page 69). When correlated against the behaviours parent/ carers report (detailed within Section 3) it is evident that all children detailed by their parent/carer, within this 2018 CPVA survey, who engage in CPVA, do meet the criteria for a diagnosis of Conduct Disorder under both ICD-10/ ICD-11 and DSM-V, as shown in Table 2 (page 69):

| TABLE 1 | | | |
|---|---|---|---|
| Aggression to people and animals | Destruction of property | Deceitfulness or theft | Serious violations of rules |
| 1. Often bullies, threatens, or intimidates others | 8. Has deliberately set fires with intention to cause serious damage | 10. Broken into someone else's house or car | 13. Stays out at night despite parental objections (beginning before age 13) |
| 2. Often initiates physical fights | 9. Deliberately destroyed the property of others | 11. Often lies to obtain goods or favours, or to avoid obligations | 14. Has run away from home at least twice for an extended period of time |
| 3. Has used a dangerous weapon that can harm others | | 12. Steals items of a nontrivial value without confronting the victim | 15. Often truant from school (beginning before age 13) |
| 4. Has been physically cruel to others | | | |
| 5. Has been physically cruel to animals | | | |
| 6. Has stolen while confronting a victim | | | |
| 7. Has forced someone into sexual activity | | | |

(American Psychiatric Association, 2013)

| TABLE 2 | Behaviours reported | within the 2018 CPVA | survey |
|---|---|---|---|
| Aggression to people and animals | Destruction of property | Deceitfulness or theft | Serious violations of rules |
| 1. Often bullies, threatens, or intimidates others | 8. Has deliberately set fires with intention to cause serious damage | 10. Broken into someone else's house or car | 13. Stays out at night despite parental objections (beginning before age 13) |
| 2. Often initiates physical fights | 9. Deliberately destroyed the property of others | 11. Often lies to obtain goods or favors, or to avoid obligations | 14. Has run away from home at least twice for an extended period of time |
| 3. Has used a dangerous weapon that can harm others | | 12. Steals items of a nontrivial value without confronting the victim | 15. Often truant from school (beginning before age 13) |
| 4. Has been physically cruel to others | | | |
| 5. Has been physically cruel to animals | | | |
| 6. Has stolen while confronting a victim | | | |
| 7. Has forced someone into sexual activity | | | |

Within the responses received for the 2018 CPVA survey and detailed across section 3, parent/carer reports point to at least 5-6 behaviours on average, that is more than the number required to enable the child to be diagnosed with a conduct Disorder under ICD-10/ ICD-11 (World Health Organisation, 2016 and 2018) and DSM-V. Moreover, this clearly places CPVA, without intention, under the care of Health professional rather than 'law' professionals, as is the current situation within England, Wales and Northern Ireland, due to the abusive nature of the 'criminal' behaviour, that in turn requires the Home Office to respond with relevant Guidance and Regulations. Home Office (2015) Guidance then points for a need to 'Police' CPVA as a domestic abuse concern, completely removing this from a Health indicator. In situating CPVA within Mental Health conditions, the need to edit the current Child Safety Order specification is negated and allows those responding, including the Police, to refer the family to Health service providers for support and intervention. Allowing for CPVA to be distinguished within the DSM-V perimeters as a Conduct Disorder, or more specifically the World Health Organisation ICD-10/ ICD-11 F91-0 *Conduct disorder confined to family context* also synchronises with the proposed age of onset for CPVA commencing; in that, the DSM-V clearly states, Conduct Disorders can appear as *'early as pre-school'* with *'Oppositional Defiance Disorder'* as a common pre-morbid condition, that may progress to Conduct Disorder. They continue within the DSM-V to note that middle childhood to adolescence is the time frame most Conduct Disorders manifest which clearly resonates the indicators reported within the 2018 CPVA survey detailed within section 3; not only that of behaviour displayed but also the onset age indicated. The category of Conduct Disorder diagnoses is categorised into three areas: the first is when 'youth' shows one characteristic of Conduct Disorder prior to age 10, the second reflects Adolescent onset with no pre-indicator before age 10 and the third is where there are sufficient indicators to diagnose but no determinant age of onset. Alongside the potential for CPVA to be recognised as a Conduct Disorder, outside of any co-morbid diagnosis, then allows Intermittent Explosive Disorder to be considered and applied rather than CPVA (or any derivative term such as Violent Child Behaviour (VCB), Adolescent to Parent Violence (APV), Adolescent to Parent Abuse (APA) and so on). The need to move from discussing CPVA as a holistic perspective, depicting any violent or aggressive behaviour displayed by children, to discussing IED (intermittent Explosive Disorder) as the new definition, provides the clear distinction between CPVA (with intent) as it is known and CPVA (without intent).

According to the American Psychiatric Association (2013) Intermittent Explosive Disorder involves impulsive or anger-based outburst of behaviour that start rapidly and are out of proportion to any trigger indicator. They go onto clarify that

> The outbursts often last fewer than 30 minutes and are provoked by minor actions of someone close, often a family member or friend. The aggressive episodes are generally _impulsive and/or based in anger rather than premeditated_. They typically occur with significant distress or psychosocial functional impairment. Aggressiveness must be "grossly out of proportion" to the provocation and accompanying psychosocial stressors (ibid) (my emphaisis)

However, the most significant aspect of considering CPVA to actually be Intermittent Explosive Disorder is the definition not only of the behaviour, but of the intention; whereby the American Psychiatric Association (2013) state that the behaviour *'has very little build up'* and *'The recurrent outbursts are neither premeditated, nor are they to achieve an outcome. Thus, outbursts are impulsive or based in anger, and are not meant to intimidate or to seek money or power'*. This reflects the main area of disagreement to date over CPVA for many families, in that the parent/ carer themselves emphasis that they do not feel their child's behaviour is intentional. Correlating the data generated within parent/carer responses for the 2018 CPVA survey, and reflecting on previous research findings, would suggest the is a clear distinction between intentional CPVA and non-intentional CPVA, suggesting that non-intentional CPVA is recognised within Conduct Disorders as Intermittent Explosive Behaviour. The American Psychiatric Association (2013) outline two types of Intermittent Explosive Behaviour. The first type of types of Intermittent Explosive Behaviour is outlined as:

> 'characterized by episodes of verbal and/or non-damaging, nondestructive, or non-injurious physical assault that occur, on average, twice weekly for three months, These could include temper tantrums, tirades, verbal arguments/fights, or assault without damage. This criterion includes high frequency/low intensity outbursts'

This reference provides the basis for recording episodes of behaviour in younger children, when it is not 'just temper tantrums' but something 'more', at a time when violent or aggressive behaviour commences and the majority of this is verbal aggression rather than physical aggression, or behaviour displayed by those children under school age. The second type of Intermittent Explosive Behaviour is outlined as:

*'is characterized by more severe destructive/assaultive episodes that are more infrequent and occur, on average, three times within a twelve-month period. These could be destroying an object without regard to its value or assaulting a person or an animal. This criterion includes high-intensity/low-frequency outbursts.'*

The second type resonates with parent/ carers arguments that, without intervention and support, the behaviour displayed does escalate and does become entrenched. Such behaviour is outlined in all reports to date seeking to understand CPVA, with specific reference to children over the age of 10 years especially during adolescence. To determine diagnosis, the DSM-V outlines that the child must be unable to control their violent or aggressive behaviour that includes *'Verbal aggression like temper tantrums, tirades, arguments or fights; or physical aggression toward people, animals, or property'* and as highlighted within Table 3, these children do fulfil this requirement to meet the diagnosis of Intermittent Explosive Behaviour. Furthermore, the DSM-V handbook (American Psychiatric Association, 2013) outlines that the following requirements are met with reference to this lack of control:

- This aggression must occur, on average, twice per week for three months.
- The physical aggression does not damage or destroy property, nor does it physically injure people or animals. **or**

Within 12 months, three behavioral outbursts resulting in:

- Damage or destruction of property, and/or
- Physical assault that physically injures people or animals.
                         (American Psychiatric Association, 2013)

These pre-requisite needs are clearly demonstrated within Section 3 and Section 4. Whilst diagnosis of Intermittent Explosive Disorder is limited to children aged six years or more, earlier indicators should be recorded to help support the evidence base for Intermittent Explosive Disorder to be confirmed when the child reaches 6 years of age, if under 6 years of age when concerns are initially raised. However, with reference to parent/ carers own suggestions the majority age for the onset of CPVA is at 6 years of age, as illustrated in research to date including this report, therefore these parents/ carers should also be advised to keep a record diary of incidents, including type (type 1 or type 2) frequency and category (as outlined within table 3).

**Section Summary**

This section argues that the current status quo of identifying children via an Educational Health Care Plan, as those needing support and intervention, wholly fails those children who 'manage' in school but require specific targeted support for emotional regulation. Within this section the relationship between emotional regulation as an internalised and externalised behaviour, that impacts upon children who are Looked After or have been Previously Looked After[33] or a child with SEND, which can lead to displays of CPVA is highlighted. Furthermore, this section points to reasons why CPVA can become entrenched or escalate as a consequence of being overlooked. Additionally, this section notes that current studies correlating parenting approaches with CPVA overlook therapeutic parenting, an approach that is an essential aspect of family life for those with a child that is Looked After or Previously Looked[34] or a child with SEND. Likewise, family typologies may enable research to be focused on CPVA in specific groups of families, but this does not reflect the internal and external influences upon children and young people in a more technological age; that has been seen by many as the most powerful influence on children's mental health and wellbeing at this time. To progress from current understanding research may need to focus more readily on society overall, rather than family typologies, and adopt a more holistic approach to the child; recognising how the child or young person perceives their world as an indicator for any CPVA occurring. If internal and external impact is a prominent indicator of CPVA then how children and young people engage with their world, and perceive their world externally, is an essential component of developing intervention approaches. In the 21$^{st}$ century, the impact of technological advances needs to be recognised in any discussion relating to how children perceive their world. Furthermore, how technological advances impact directly as an internal and external influence on children's perceptions has to be included if understanding of children's worlds is to be achieved. Children are being introduced to technology as a means of communication and socialisation and therefore technology plays an intrinsic part of children's worlds. This factor is important given the increased use of media and social networks by children that can escalate the CPVA behaviours children display if they were subject to online bullying for example[35]. Such indicators

---

[33] including children who are adopted, living with family members (Special Guardianship or Kinship).
[34] including children who are adopted, living with family members (Special Guardianship or Kinship).
[35] from 2011 to 2017, when Ofcom (2017) produced their report into children and parent's media use and attitudes. Ofcom *(ibid.)* indicated that as many as one in four 8-11-year olds and three in four 12-15-year olds had a social media presence; particularly within social platforms that had age restrictions. Following on from engagement

support argument that considering the individual child or young person, and how they internalise and externalise their world, is a fundamental aspect of understanding CPVA increases; in that many children may report via social media platforms or 'chat rooms' violence within the home, which in turn could be viewed as domestic violence between adult and adult if the child is not clear about who is displaying the violence. This section supports new suggestions that there is an indicative need to address Adverse Childhood Experiences in any future studies of CPVA. The potential correlation between internal and external circumstance was employed by Simmons et al (2018) when they reviewed 60 years of CPVA indicators. Using Bronfenbrenner's (1979) ecological model of development they were able to include multi-factor holistic positions, that allowed for a variety of indicators to be considered, reflective of the work of Perry's Neurosequential model of Therapeutics (1998 and 2006) and the findings of the Adverse Childhood Experiences; that enables CPVA to be viewed as a *"by-product of an interaction between specific kinds of individual, situational, and biological factors"* (Simmons et al. 2018 p.31). This proposal by Simmons et al (*(ibid)* resonates with discussion to date, that CPVA is not a consequence of a single theory that have supported suggestions of CPVA associated to family typology or 'poor parenting' or gender specific. They concluded that

> *"In the 60 years since the first scientific study of CPA, our understanding of what it looks like and why it occurs remains fragmented and poorly developed. This is largely due to a weak theoretical foundation for much of the existing research, limited consideration of the multiple determinants of aggressive behavior, and the use of operational variables that do not reflect theoretical constructs"* (Simmons et al 2018 p.43)

reflecting the summary of discussion into CPVA and moving these discussions from single theory positions to multi-faceted positions; which incorporate the myriad of factors that reflect children's worlds in situ. More concerningly this section highlights that for many parents the reality of not being supported by an EHCP, for the child who engages in CPVA, to provide the support and interventions they need; leaves these families with little alternative other than:

---

with media, the NSPCC pointed to over 12,000 counselling sessions with young people who talk to Childline about online issues during 2016-2017 all of which could become 'triggers' for CPVA behaviour in the home.

- seek support via a Section 20 when behaviour escalates to such an extent they are no longer able to manage the child and keep the child safe at home **or**

- seek a Section 20 due to the child displaying CPVA posing a real risk of harm to a sibling (or others within the family) **or**

- seek police intervention via the criminal system if the child is over 10 years of age **or**

- self-fund support **or**

- simply 'put up and shut up' **or**

- Request a referral to CAMHS (Child and Adolescent Mental Health Services) and be placed on the waiting list, which can be for more than 6 months before the 1st appointment.

Within this section, there is clear evidence that when reporting CPVA this should be classified within Conduct Disorders as determined by both ICD-10/ ICD-11 (World Health Organisation, 2016 and 2018) and DSM-V (American Psychiatric Association, 2013). Whilst the majority of parent/ carers participating in the 2018 CPVA survey report their child does have a diagnosed condition, no participant included the area in which CPVA clearly meets the pre-requisite needs for diagnosis as a co-morbid condition.

Diagnosing CPVA as a Conduct Disorder under the categories and definitions outlined within ICD-10/ ICD-11 and DSM-V places CPVA within Mental Health provision, rather than the current perception of being a 'criminal' offence; this in turn moves CPVA outside of any Home Office guidance if the CPVA displayed is without intent. If this recommendation is made then this provides a significant step forward in supporting the child, their parent/carer and all family members within the home environment, by clearly recognising that

1. It is not the 'fault' of the parent or due to 'poor parenting'
2. It is not intentional or preconceived.

Such clarification is important if addressing the issue of CPVA and understanding the relationship between CPVA and SEND, by recognising CPVA may reflect the diagnosis of Intermittent Explosive Disorder and is therefore a co-morbid Conduct Disorder in its own right, rather than as a behaviour trait of any other Conduct Disorder. In this way CPVA without intent needs to be evidenced as Intermittent Explosive Disorder that can diagnosed as a co-morbid condition in much the same way as anxiety and depression can be separately determined but resonate at the same time as co-morbidity indicators. Furthermore, Intermittent Explosive Disorder has previously been outlined alongside Post Traumatic Stress Disorder as well as Attention Deficit Hyperactivity Disorder, therefore this approach needs to be applied accordingly to children as well as adults. Establishing the behaviour as Intermittent Explosive Disorder provides the pathway for support for parent/ carers to be forthcoming. Whilst it is also recognised that some children, particularly in adolescence **intend** to behave in a manner that is reflective of CPVA, according to the current definition, not only planning this but intend to behave violently or aggressively, the majority of children **do not intend** to do so. It is therefore pertinent that any professional working with a family who report CPVA ascertains at the outset if the child has any diagnosed Mental or Behavioural Disorders and considers the indicators for the family under the criteria of *Conduct disorder confined to family context* (WHO, 2018) ICD-10/ ICD-11 F91-0.

# Section 5. Let's Talk About:
# The cost for families living with CPVA.

The impact and consequential affect living with Child to Parent Violence or Aggression has on families is multi-faceted and permeates all areas of the lives of those within the home where CPVA occurs.  As outlined by Thorley and Coates (2017c) the actual impact, affect and cost of CPVA cannot be known, due to the level of vagueness around identifying what CPVA is and those families experiencing CPVA. A further difficulty arises when distinguishing between the direct impact, the effect and/ or the economic cost of CPVA to families and to society; for example, if injuries are reported as accidents rather than as a result of violent behaviour, or if broken items go unreported, then these costs are not assimilated as part of CPVA. With recognition to the difficulties posed, when considering how much living with CPVA costs families, there are some general areas that are recognised; some of which are direct costs others are associated costs that can include:

❖ Treatment costs for injuries sustained by health service personnel or self-treated with purchased items such as Elastoplast, bandages and so forth

❖ Treatment costs for mental health impact such as depression and anxiety provided by health services of all family members or to family if privately accessed, or to voluntary sector if opting to use a voluntary mental health service provider

❖ Loss of earnings to both the parent and their employer

❖ Loss of earnings for the family if employment change is required such as going part-time or if withdrawing from the employment marketplace

❖ Potential need to claim benefits due to loss of earnings placing a cost on government departments

❖ Repair costs and replacement costs which may lead to insurance claims for damage to property or possessions

❖ Educational costs to schools for managing 'behaviour' indicators

❖ Long term costs as outlined within ACE study findings for all family members with reference to long term Health indicators

❖ Legal costs including Youth Justice costs for the police, courts and associated legal teams.

Whilst the cost of CPVA may remain unknown overall, there are proposed indicators of how much domestic violence costs society within the UK, calculated as direct and indirect costs. Such costing estimates of domestic violence reflect adult-adult violence or aggression but may provide insight into potential costs for families living with CPVA, as a form of domestic violence. The cost of domestic violence to society is notably substantive, Woman's Aid considered suggestions by Walby (2009) and pointed to the collective cost of domestic abuse to be £15.73 billion per year, if this included

- services (such as police, doctors, social workers and so forth),
- loss of economic output (from employment or withdrawal from employment) along with
- human and emotional costs (including treatment for depression, anxiety and so forth).

Whilst it is not proposed the cost of CPVA is to the same level or scale of that for Domestic Violence involving adult to adult, there needs to be recognition of the real cost to families who live with CPVA in the home. Living with CPVA incurs both a human cost and an economic cost that should not be overlooked. Wilcox et al (2015) outlined that there were substantial costs where CPVA occurs but are not fully recognised, acknowledged or addressed. They calculated that over a 6-month period[36] the cost could be as much as £195, 362 for 8 families. Using this cost base as a base line for providing 'Break4change' as an intervention strategy programme, for 8 families, at a cost of £2,297 per family, they argued that for every 8 families engaging in the programme a saving of £48,840 could be generated, from future costs of supporting families living with CPVA (as detailed within Table 3, page 86). Such savings for 8 families could then be multiplied over the number of families who require this, which could be several thousand families within England, Ireland, Scotland and Wales.

---

[36] an estimate of savings calculated over a 6 month period (costings from the Troubled Families Negative Cost Savings)

| Table 3 | |
|---|---|
| **Savings** | **Euros** |
| Criminal Justice System | 79,305 |
| Health Services | 15,245 |
| Children and Families Services: <br> Children in Care, Foster Care, Social Work, School Savings to Services | 97,691 |
| Housing and Homeless | 3,121 |
| **Total Savings Over 6 Months** | **195,362** |
| Cost per family per Break4Change programme (intervention strategy programme) | 2,297 |
| **Projected saving per 8 families** | **48,840** |

These costs do not include the human cost for families living with CPVA, which is estimated by those living with CPV to be substantially more. The cost to families is considerable on an individual level and a collective level, which in turn feeds into the cost to society for supporting families living with CPVA. It is therefore essential when discussing CPVA to consider the real-world cost for families. Such real-world cost needs to acknowledge any support network that these families can access or lack thereof. To provide insight into the real cost of living with CPVA, the CPVA 2018 survey asked respondents about impact upon their relationships, employment, emotional well-being and household finances. Within the responses generated it is striking that only 3% of families felt that there had been no impact on their relationships either within their family, or wider afield, as a direct consequence of living with a child or children who engage in CPVA. As such this means that 97% of families felt that their relationships with others had been affected, irrespective of whether this was a couple family or single parent family, a birth parent family or a 'blended child' based family. For the majority of families, the impact on their relationships with others was a concurrent impact, involving their relationship with their partner, other children in the home, wider family relatives such as grandparents, as well as friendship groups; something that is clearly evident in Chart 11.

Chart 11: The impact of CPVA on parent's relaitonships with partners, other children in the home, the wider family and friends

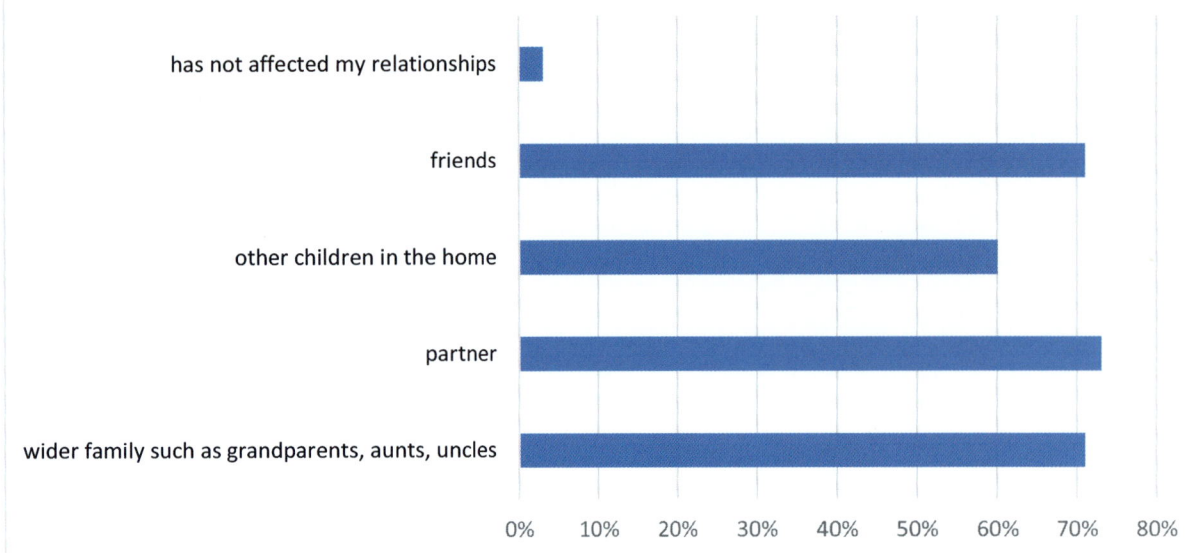

|  |  |
|---|---|
| has not affected my relationships | |
| friends | |
| other children in the home | |
| partner | |
| wider family such as grandparents, aunts, uncles | |

0%  10%  20%  30%  40%  50%  60%  70%  80%

Such indicators highlight how and why, families living with CPVA can become isolated within society; through the potential withdrawal of emotional support from partners, wider family members or friends. Paradoxically, it is at this time, of living with CPVA behaviour in the home, that these parents are in need of a supportive relationship from their partner, wider family members and friends. Such support is essential to maintain the parents own mental wellbeing and to reduce the magnitude of the impact of living with CPVA; including any feelings of guilt, failure or shame that these parents may feel.  What is interesting within the findings generated is where the impact on parental/ carer relationships with other children in the home is placed, whilst this is still notable (60% of responses received) the impact on siblings was reported to a lesser degree than that of any other relationship impact that the parent/ carer had with others, by at least 10%. It is evident that participating parent/ carers felt there was a significantly larger impact on their relationships with other adults in their lives, as opposed to other children; irrespective of if this was their partner, their wider family members or their friendship group. One reason may be that the other child or children within the home also engage in CPVA, therefore the relationship is already complicated in its own right. An alternative reason may be that parent/ carer endeavours to retain their relationships with other children, prioritising this relationship over that with their partner, wider family members or friends. In this way parent/ carers may expend more energy and focus on their relationship with other children, rather than other adults in their lives, in order to protect such relationship's.  A further consideration, when reflecting on the overall data, needs to also account for those families with only one child in the home. For those parent/ carer respondents, who live with only one child, there would not be an impact on their relationship with any other child in the home by default (insomuch as there are no other children in the home). To determine the level of impact by sub-group, the findings were interrogated by the following indicators, and then correlated against the impact on relationships for these specific sub-group categories specifically:

| Couple parent sub group | | Single parent sub group |
|---|---|---|
| Adopter couple with 1 child | | Adopter single parent with 1 child |
| Birth couple with 1 child | | Birth single parent with 1 child |
| Adopter couple with 2 children | | Adopter single parent with 2 children |
| Birth couple with 2 children | | Birth single parent with 2 children |
| Adopter couple with 3 children | | Adopter single parent with 3 children |
| Birth Couple with 3 children | | Birth single parent with 3 children |
| Adopter couple with 4/5 children | | Adopter single parent with 4/5 children |
| Birth couple with 4/5 children | | Birth single parent with 4/5 children |

Due to the different number of responses in each sub-group, the findings were interrogated as a percentage of that particular group for comparison purposes. This provided insight into how living with CPVA had impacted upon the relationships of these sub-group families specifically, as detailed within Chart 12

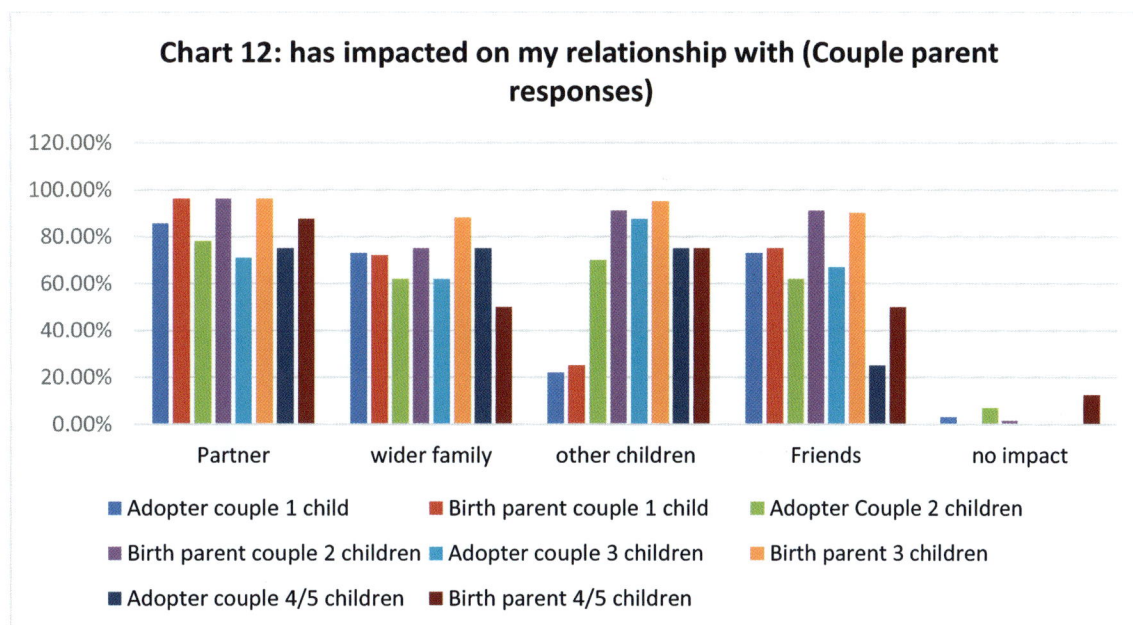

Chart 12: has impacted on my relationship with (Couple parent responses)

Separating the findings into more detailed analysis highlights the level of significance living with CPVA has upon the couple's relationship with their partner. The level of impact is notable across all family sub-groups, but more so for birth parent couples than that of adoptive couples; irrespective of how many children reside in the family home. One explanation is where a child with SEND displays CPVA, in that it has been previously suggested those families living with children who have SEND are at higher risk of separation and divorce than those families living with children who do not have SEND, for example: Wymbs *et al* (2008) pointed to an increase of 22.7% of parents of children with ADHD had divorced prior to the child's 8th birthday (the significance of which was that there was no increase if they remained married beyond the child's 8th birthday). This was also reflected in Hartley *et al's* (2010) study, involving children with Autism, where there was an increased risk of separation or divorce to that of their peers (23.5% compared to 13.8%). Similarly, Robbers *et al* (2011) reflected on a sample of 6,400 children who were identified as experiencing internalising/ externalising problems at age 3 years old; following which, they reported that there appeared to be a correlation between higher levels of externalising problems (aggression, conduct disorders and Hyperactivity) in girls at age 3 (but not boys) that could in turn predict later parental separation or divorce. These indicators are also evident in children under 5 who display CPVA. However, such argument is disputed in recent evidence, for example Claudette-Jean Girard, Attorney at Law posted in Family Law on August 12th 2016 that the evidence of indication is flawed and went onto state that:

> *While these studies, undoubtedly, have a point that raising a special-needs child has its stressors and challenges, a new study was released that could challenge the traditional view on this issue. The Kennedy Krueger Institute, which studies autism and related disorders, found that 64 percent of children with an autism spectrum disorder (ASD) belong to a family with two married biological or adoptive parents, compared with 65 percent of children who do not have an ASD. Essentially, the rate of divorce was pretty much identical in parents who did or did not have a child with autism or a related disorder.*

This points to a cumulative impact for these families, not only that of supporting a child with SEND but also a child with SEND who engages in CPVA. Following this suggestion, CPVA may then be part of a myriad of reasons why the parent/ carer feels there is a significant impact on their relationship with their partner. Subsequently, some families may feel the impact on their relationship with their partner is associated with the child's overall SEND need, rather than the child's engagement in CPVA specifically, in that the CPVA displayed is part of the overall behavioural condition and not a separate entity. It is also possible that adopter families have different expectations for their child's behaviour, that has been developed through discussion with other adopters, or as part of their adoption preparation programme. In this way adopters may reflect the child's behaviour to be the after-effect of the child's pre-adoption experiences. On a more personal level it may be parents, who are adopters, attribute the child's behaviour as 'not of my doing' in that they themselves did not cause the child's earlier 'trauma' experiences; and in this way feel it is 'not my fault'. Using this argument recognises that for birth parents the child's earlier experiences are developed within the family home, not elsewhere in any other family home, therefore birth parents may develop a sense of 'poor parenting' or self-blame for their child's behaviour more readily.  Alternatively, birth parents may disagree about why the child engages in CPVA and blame each other, or reflect the behaviour as something they need to manage, due to the child's SEND diagnosis, thereby accepting the behaviour as part of that diagnosis.

**The cost of living with CPVA for Couple parent sub-groups**

The indication of a higher impact for birth parent couples, compared to adopter parent couples, is not seen as consistently within the parent's relationship and wider family members (illustrated in Chart 12), in that the impact on relationships with wider family members for both adopter couples and birth parent couples, with 1 child in the home, is almost identical. However, for those family couples with 2 children in the home, the impact on relationships with wider family members is notably greater (by 15%) for birth family couples, than it is for adopter family couples, a finding that is more so when there are 3 children in the home. There are many reasons why this may occur, for example this may reflect the parent's previous relationship with their 'in-laws', prior to the CPVA behaviour being displayed. For all families, difficulties can arise from wider family member understanding of the child's position, such as the life history of those children who are adopted, or the diagnosis of SEND for those children with SEND. Wider family members may have preconceived ideas developed over time about what the behaviour should be, for those children diagnosed with SEND or for those children who were Previously Looked After (such as adopted children). Their perception will have developed from societal expectations, which can differ greatly to the reality of parenting individual children with individual needs. For older members of the wider family, they may base their expectations of the child against their own personal experience of parenting, that in itself can create further difficulty. In this way difficulties can also arise when wider family members look to the 'in law' parent to be at fault; or for those who have adopted, look to the parents to reflect a more traditional parenting approach, rather than a therapeutic parenting approach, to manage the child's behaviour (irrespective of the child's previous family history or experience or trauma). The difference between the impact on relationships with wider family members appears to be more than 25% greater for birth parents with 3 children, than that of adopter parents with 3 children, a finding that is reversed if there are 4/5 children in the home. Further investigation should be carried out to understand the wider implications of this impact, given grandparents provide a substantial amount of family/ kinship care across society at this time; for example, providing school run cover or babysitting or childcare. Without this wider family support many families struggle to be part of society, or may feel greater shame, embarrassment and isolation, that in turn has a detrimental impact upon the whole family.

The impact on birth parent couples continues to be higher than that on adopter couple families for other children in the home, that in turn can intermix with other relationships these birth families are struggling with. Irrespective of how many children reside in the home, across all groups, a higher number of birth parents report living with CPVA impacts on their relationship with other children in the home; particularly for those families with 2 or 3 children. However, as the number of children increases to 4/5 children in the home, the impact for both birth parent couples and adopter parent couples is similar, with little difference between these family sub-groups. One explanation may relate to the amount of time children displaying CPVA are shown, as the focus of the parent's attention and input, compared to other children in the home. For the safety of all children, parents may need to focus significant amounts of time with the child who engages in CPVA exclusively and by default have less time to spend with any other children in the home exclusively. Additionally, it may be that parents are limited in the outings and activities they can engage and participate in as a family group, due to concerns the parent/ carer may have, relating to how the child displaying CPVA will behave during the outing or activity. Such indicators have been noted previously, particularly for those families living with a child who has behavioural SEND[37]. This selective process can restrict activities for other children in the home and cause resentment, if

---

[37] see for example: Rogers, 2007; Reichman *et al*, 2008; Contact a Family, 2011; Moorhead, 2013; Disability Planet, n.d.; Scope, 2014; National Disability Authority, 2014

priority is given to the child who engages in CPVA. The impact upon relationships, particularly that which affects the parent/ carer relationship with any other children living in the home, supports indicators proposed by Selwyn *et al* (2014). Selwyn pointed to a higher level of Previously Looked After Children (specifically Adopted for their study) had been placed into the care of the Local Authority by parents for a range of factors, including the impact upon the parent's relationship with other children in the home.  This action is not an easy decision to reach, however it may be that this option is better known to adopter couples than that of birth parents, who may have very little understanding or previous contact with Statutory Service representatives. This is not to imply such decisions are easier for adopter couples, they are not, if anything such decisions can lead to adopter couples experiencing significant trauma themselves. Within the 2018 CPVA survey respondents were asked if the child displaying CPVA continued to reside within the home environment; of which 6% indicated that the child no longer lived at home. For these families the main deciding factor was due to escalating violence, alongside a need to establish safety within the home, as stated by these families including:

- *Violence to us - the increasing violence became impossible to endure*
- *Threatening behaviour constantly with tension in home never leaving*
- *Allegations reason for leaving, violence prevented return*
- *We could no longer keep our family safe*
- *She tried to commit suicide. A high court judge then ruled that she was to immediately reside at our chosen school*
- *Family life is intolerable and unsafe. Over 30 police call outs*
- *To enable child to get help and support for autism*
- *I couldn't keep him or other child safe when he was distressed or absconding, and no support forthcoming*
- *Threatening behaviour and constantly running away therefore we felt unable to keep child safe*
- *Tried to throw my husband down the stairs-removed by police for our protection then put in voluntary foster care*
- *Her behaviour became intolerable.  She smashed up her room and was violent and aggressive. She was arrested.  We dropped charges since we did not want her to have a criminal record- we want her to have help.  She was mad because we "wasted her time"! She wanted to move out - we arranged it for her.  The situation was intolerable. She was suicidal and was absconding and we had police involved. The stress was unbearable*
- *Had a period of time living with grandparents following a physical attack on me but child attacked grandparents*
- *He physically threatened to burn the house down. I had him arrested and refused to let him come home.*
- *My wife and I could no longer cope with the aggression!*
- *Her violence, threats to kill me and danger to herself*

- *Physical and emotional abuse directed at a sibling and emotional abuse towards myself.*
- *My youngest son who is aggressive is at home but my eldest son (birth child) has chosen to go to a boarding school to cope with the dynamics in the family now (he is not violent/aggressive)*

Such indicators and reports, from parent/ carers, emphasise the emotional cost of living with CPVA on family units, demonstrating how living with a child who displays CPVA has a compound impact on the family overall, that is complex and multifarious; one that extends within the home environment and beyond to wider family and friendship groups.

The impact on friendship groups for parents living with CPVA adds to the existing difficulties these families experience. With the exception of couple parents living with 1 child in the home, birth parents are significantly more likely to report an impact on their relationships with friends, that is clearly noted within chart 12. There are many reasons why more birth parents than adopters may report an impact on their relationship with friends, including having less time to spend with friends for example: if the child displaying CPVA has SEND and requires a significant amount of time, or a sense of guilt/ shame/ embarrassment for being unable to control their child's behaviour compared to how a 'friend' manages their own children; a factor noted by Brule and Eckstein (2016 p.2-3) who highlighted that

> "Abused parents recognize and often internalize larger societal messages— communicated by professionals and popular culture—surrounding "good" versus "bad" parents. "Good parents" discipline and provide structure for their children— proper parental behaviors expected to cause well-behaved, respectful, and morally strong offspring. Stigma of "bad AtPA[38] parents" involves societal attributional labels that they: use improper parenting techniques, are uneducated and uninformed as to healthy parenting skills, and prefer to let children disrespect and abuse, rather than dealing with their problems"

This explains the difficulties these parents have in seeking support, and how or why their own relationships with partners, other children in the home, wider family members and friends may experience significant difficulties, following the onset of CPVA behaviour. Brule and Eckstein (2016, p.2-3) continue and suggest that *"These parents are constituted as having "transgresse[d] the 'reciprocality'" of parenting relationships as well as the "normative developmental transitions" framing "expectations of when and how"* child-adult roles should

---

[38] AtPA is one of the acronyms used for Adolescence to Parent Abuse

*be enacted"*. Providing explanation why difficulties can and do arise for parents living with CPVA with reference to their relationships with others. Wider family and friends may struggle to accommodate that the parent is unable to control the behaviour of their own child, particularly if this is based on the wider family, or friends, own parenting experiences (and experience that will formulate from their own understanding of society, cultural/ family expectations and family/ cultural values). In this way partners, other children in the home or wider family, may express more tolerance of those children who are 'Looked After' or have been 'Previously Looked After' if they anticipate the child/ children to have behavioural issues prior to placement, based on their perception of who these children are. The suggestion of preconception may explain why more adopter couples than birth family couples responded to indicate that there was no impact on their relationship's overall. However, it is worth noting that whilst both adopter and birth parents pointed to no impact on their relationships overall, these respondents represent a small percentage of the overall sub-group type and for the majority of parents, there is a significant impact.

**The cost of living with CPVA for Single parent sub-groups**

The cost of living with CPVA is not isolated to couple families, single parent families also report an impact on their relationships with partners, other children in the home and wider family. Whilst it may be anticipated, or within the 'norm', to expect couple families to experience difficulties in their relationship with their partner, this is not exclusive to only couple parents, as detailed within Chart 13:

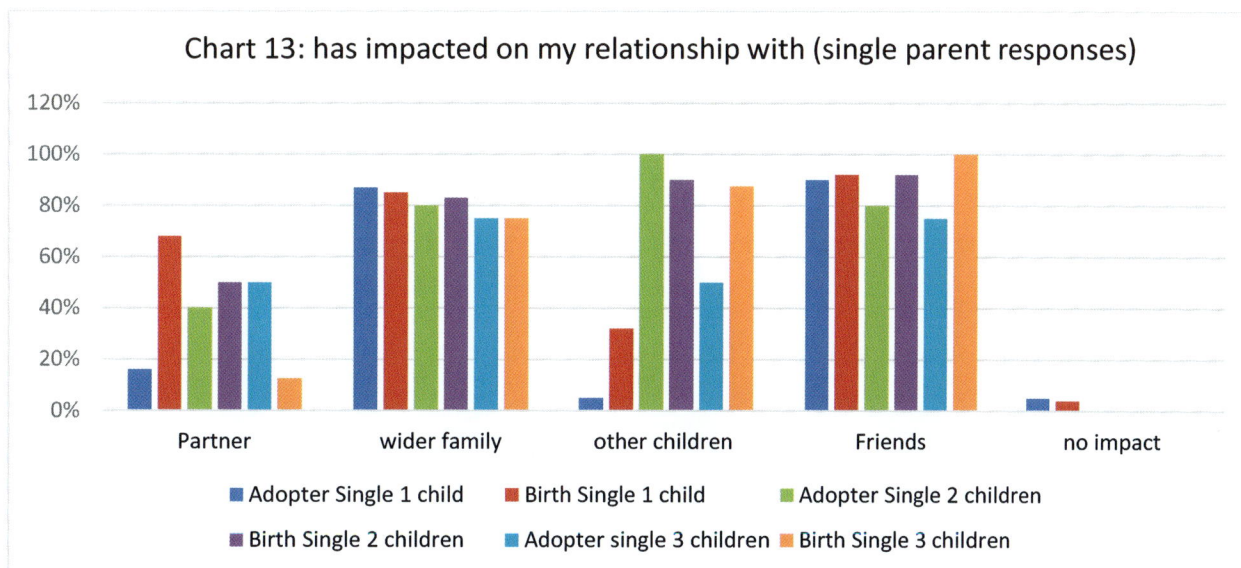

Chart 13: has impacted on my relationship with (single parent responses)

Legend: Adopter Single 1 child, Birth Single 1 child, Adopter Single 2 children, Birth Single 2 children, Adopter single 3 children, Birth Single 3 children

As noted within Chart 13, there is a significant difference between how living with CPVA impacts upon partner relationships for those parents who adopt one child, compared to birth parents with one child (of more than 52%). One reason explaining this impact is the level of existing partner relationships prior to the child arriving in the family home; insomuch as single 'adopters', having applied to become a single adopter, are less likely to be in a partner relationship as such prior to adoption (being in a relationship or co-habiting may point to couple adoption rather than single parent adoption applications). Alternatively, 'birth' parents are more likely to be in a relationship prior to the arrival of the 'birth' child; although this relationship may not last for the duration of the pregnancy. Moreover, whilst birth parents may not co-habit with each other, the child's co-parent may still feature in the child's life. Furthermore, it is feasible that the relationship between partners becomes untenable following their experience of living with a child with SEND that includes CPVA, so much so the parents separated or divorced; leaving the remaining parent as a single parent at the point of participating in the 2018 CPVA survey. For single parents with 2 children within the home the difference living with CPVA has had on their relationship with partners is not so notable; however, when living with 3 children in the home the impact upon adopter relationships with partners, compared to that of birth parents, is notable. For adopter parents living with 3 children there is a significantly higher impact on their relationship with their partner than that of birth parents living with 3 children. Such indicators require more considered investigation to establish how many of these single parents have become so following the onset of CPVA within the family home; whereby the co-parent has left the family home unable to continue to reside with a child or children displaying CPVA. With reference to the impact on relationships with wider family, as seen in couple parent families, 70-80% of those responding pointed to a definitive impact with wider family members.  Reasons for this can reflect those outlined for couple parent households, additionally for any single parent families, where the relationship with a partner did become untenable (leading to separation or divorce) there is the potential for a cascade impact with wider family members who were previously 'in laws'.

A further aspect that can impact upon single parent families and create a negative impact, in all of their relationships, is that of the 'stigma' of being a single parent within society; including cultural or societal presumptions associated with single parenthood. Wider family members may be sensitive to how society perceive the single parent overall, as a reflection of societal expectations; that contradict or conflict with how the single parent perceives their own position in society. The impact of stigma is outlined within Brule and Eckstein (2016 p.2-3)

> *The moral stigma of character deficits, although privately maintained, is ever-present for parents who are seen by self and any knowing others as having failed in their child-rearing **and -relationship responsibilities**. Because they must perpetually manage identity-privacy boundaries, moral or character stigmas are particularly stressful for those who try to conceal the problem..(of AtPA- my emphasis)*

It is interesting that 22% of single adopter parents and 25% of single birth parents note an impact on their relationship with other children in the home, so much so that further investigation in any future studies would be warranted, to establish who the additional children are that reside in the home. For single adopter parents it is those parents with 2 children who are more likely to point to an impact upon their relationship with the other child in the home. As discussed for couple families there is an increased demand on the parent's time, energy and focus, exclusively towards the child who displays CPVA behaviour; from the onset of CPVA occurring, to after such behaviour, as well as continually during the time spent together monitoring for potential CPVA occurring. This means for these parents there may be little time left for the 2nd child within the home. For single parents, if there is no partner support at home, these single parents can struggle to provide an equal amount of focus, time and energy for the 2nd child to that of the child engaging in CPVA. This in turn can create tension or feelings of lesser importance or feelings of neglect by the 2nd child and impact directly on their relationship with their parent. Likewise, similar to those couple families living with more than one child engaging in CPVA, if a single parent is managing more than one child's CPVA behaviour, as the lone adult in the home, then the impact upon their relationship with the children in the home will be constrained. Whilst there is a similar impact upon relationships with other children in the home for single parents with 2 children, the impact on single parents with 3 children is not as equitable; whereby there is notably more birth parents pointing to an impact on their relationship with other children in the home, to that of single adopter parents, when there are more than 3 children in the home. Once again there are many reasons why this may be so, including separation or divorce or death of the co-parent. The isolation that may be experienced following separation, divorce or death of the co-parent can be compounded if there is also a loss of friendship. What is notable is the impact upon friendships for single parents, which is concerning, as this can leave these families isolated and at risk of increasing CPVA behaviours occurring, due to lack of support. For birth parents the impact on friendship ranges from 90% for those birth parents with 1 child to almost 100% for those birth parents with 3 children. Whilst adopter single parents do not point to similar levels of impact on their friendships it is still significant at 75-90%.

**The relationship cost for all families living with CPVA**

The cost to parents living with CPVA on their relationship is a very real human cost that the evidence indicates is substantial and profound. This real cost can leave families isolated which in turn can leave these parents subject to self-blame or to feel self-critical, as families who represent a range of societal stigma 'types'; this is important in that such feelings may encourage these families to continue to live with 'hidden' domestic violence rather than seek help from external avenues. The impact stigmatisation has for these families can increase the impact on their relationships with partners, other children in the home, wider family or friends; irrespective of whether they are a couple/ single parent family or adopter/ birth family, as noted by Brule and Eckstein (2016 p.2-3) who posited that:

> *Deviations from expected parental norms produce varying stigma types. AtPA can result in physical stigma, ensuing from visible-to-others bodily marks: facial/bodily/task evidence of bruises, depression, inability to concentrate, crying, and lack of sleep ... Social stigma (tribal or cultural, according to Goffman, 1963), usually associated with group characteristics, may also be a visible form of stigma for abused parents. For example, when queried as to the cause of their altered appearance or mood, parents hide or disclose their "violent family" group affiliation... Society—as shown through the goals of published studies, current laws, and lack of professional recognition/support—has little empathy for parents expected to maintain family control as authority figures...*

The cost of this relationship impact is also seen within the impact on employment for parents who live with CPVA. Couple family responses to the 2018 CPVA survey recorded that 90% of adopter couple families had seen a direct impact on their employment as a 'cost' to them. For couple parent families living with one child the impact on their employment included:

- 55% of families where one of the parent/ carers left their employment and are no longer working
- 19% of parent/ carers who had reduced their employment so that they were now working part-time.
- 22% of adopter couple parents had witnessed a real-life impact on their ability to continue with their career trajectory so much so these parents were unable to move

or progress in their employment, unable to develop their employment opportunities or professional standing or had to work restricted hours and were no longer flexible in their ability to meet employment opportunities.

A similar pattern emerged for adopter couple parent families with 2 children, where 87.5% had seen a direct impact on their employment. Within adopter couple families with 2 children, 60% of these families had seen one parent leave employment, with the remaining 27.5% adopter couple families reducing their employment hours accordingly, to either part-time or as restricted opportunities to enable them to be 'available' for the child's needs. This is significant if they had calculated their ability to accommodate two adopted children, based on a two-parent household income that was no longer a viable option. For those adopter couple families, the high level of leaving employment or living with a direct real-cost impact on their family continued across all adopter couple family groups, irrespective of how many children lived within the home, as a direct impact of living with CPVA.

The impact on employment for birth family couples mapped that of adopter families, with 94% of birth couple families noting a direct impact upon their employment and employment possibilities. The financial implications from a change in, or loss of, employment can be multi-faceted, from a reduction in lifestyle to a change of housing, all of which needs to be calculated when reflecting upon the real-life cost and impact on families living with CPVA. This is particularly important under the current economic climate, where it is well documented that there are more working families living in poverty at this time[39], how many of these working families living in poverty are also families living with CPVA, who are unable to be employed, or are restricted in their employment options, is unknown. Employability therefore needs to be considered as an essential factor when seeking to support these families and even more so for single parent families of all sub-groups. Within single parent family sub-groups

- 95% of single adopter parents with one child in the home
- 93% of single birth parents with one child in the home
- 100% of single adopter parents with 2 or more children in the home
- 93% of single birth parents with 2 or more children in the home and
- 100% of Kinship Carer/ SGOs

---

[39] It is not the purpose of this report to interrogate child poverty and working family income; however this is well documented within the Office of National Statistics data and publications relating to working families and poverty across England, Ireland and Wales, that is a trend increasing year on year.

noted a direct impact on their employment from living with CPVA, the majority of which were now no longer employed for a range of reasons including their own health and the demands of supporting the child who engaged in CPVA behaviour. Such indicators can have a cascade impact on indirect costs, if these families then need to rely on 'state welfare' support via 'benefit' payments due to the loss of income; so that the real-life cost for families living with CPVA increases. These financial costs to both family and society, as direct and indirect costs, support the argument of placing a higher level of importance on early intervention support. Early intervention, prior to the behaviour becoming entrenched or escalating, is a cost-effective measure in supporting families; whereby these families living with CPVA are not only able to retain their employment but also able to continue to be employed, without the restrictions currently impacting on their employability, resulting from living with CPVA. Furthermore, when families are able to continue in their employment they may require less 'state welfare' support in the form of benefit payment over the longer term. It therefore appears apparent that early intervention is a cost-effective strategy in economic terms, not only for the family directly but for society indirectly. The financial costs are variable and cover a wide range of areas incurred by families, including for example:

- Loss of salary
- Costs for working at home now instead of being employed including phone, heating, electricity
- Repair to broken items/ house including doors, windows, walls
- Replacement of broken items personal and home including toys, electrical items such as TV or computer and games, bikes, as well as things belonging to siblings
- Paying for professional help
- Respite such as childcare cost is substantially more for children with SEND
- Painkillers, first aid supplies for injuries
- Childcare cover for school exclusions
- Travel costs for appointments and meetings

Within these monetary costs there are extensive individual personal costs such as:

- *We have been financially crippled. Approaching £200K of debt just to keep afloat.*
- *I've lost my entire income and probably career.*

- *Had to leave work. Can't use childcare or friends for childcare. Spend a fortune on sen activities equipment courses etc.*
- *Purposefully destroyed tiles in bathroom, made holes and destroyed furniture ca £2000 damage*
- *He has stolen a lot of money that has had financial implications*
- *Hole in wall where through chair - stained glass window replaced..Replace passport and additional flight after stole sister's passport while on holiday and couldn't get home.*
- *£50 000 to £8 000 wage….*
- *Gone from 35k pa to nothing*
- *Loss of wage needed adoption allowance which I have to yearly justify with great evidence.*
- *Loss of nurse registration*

One aspect that is highlighted within responses to any potential financial impact for families living with CPVA is their appreciation of financial support from family or friends where this is given.  This support is shown through family/ friends purchasing replacement items or helping to 'loan' money to the family, as an informal loan, that enables the family living with CPVA to retain their home. However, such responses highlight the paradox of rhetoric to reality. Within England, Ireland and Wales the Department for Education outlines support for those children with SEND via the Educational Health and Care Plan framework, providing the policy rhetoric of supporting those children who have SEND. However, in reality, parent/ carer responses point to a failure in this support policy if those children identified as SEND with behaviour difficulties are being excluded from school/ education provision, as a consequence of their behaviour, that means in real terms the  parent/ carer is no longer able to maintain any employment, or be in a position of self-financing the support their child requires; this is noted within responses received: *educational costs met due to EHCP not covering this*  and was reiterated within additional responses for example: *exclusions, managed move...child at home with minimal education (1 hr a day)...so  ...employment.* A similar paradox is seen for 'Trauma' related intervention/ support/ therapy if this is not forthcoming for children who are Looked After or were Previously Looked After (irrespective of if this is Foster Care, Adopted, Kinship Care or SGO) that leaves the family to self-fund, or see the child placed into the care of the Local Authority, as detailed within the participant responses received:

> *My daughter has had to leave the family home due to her behaviour.  She is 17. We now have to pay £360/month rent, £155/term bus ticket for her to get to school since the house is not close plus money on out of house activities to see her e.g. going for lunch/cinema.  We are very lucky that we can afford this.  If not she would be back in care without a doubt.  Private therapy is also expensive.*

The loss of employment and escalating direct financial costs, alongside the impact of relationship difficulties these families may experience, can be reflected across the emotional cost of living with CPVA. As part of the cost of living with CPVA, the CPVA 2018 survey included *'It is recognised that living with child to parent aggression/ violence has an impact on parent's emotional wellbeing- do you feel this has happened to you?'* Out of the 538 responses received only 2 respondents answered 'no'. Of those indicating that there had been and impact on their emotional wellbeing, and therefore an emotional impact 'cost' to their family, over 90% indicated one or all of the following: Stress, Anxiety, Depression (for which the majority were prescribed antidepressants). In addition to these majority responses the following were also noted:

- separation/ divorce from partner
- lack of confidence in self/ lack of confidence as a parent
- frightened of child
- emotionally exhausted
- physically exhausted
- physical wellbeing impact: stomach ulcer, high blood pressure, constantly tired, weight gain
- crying/ tearful
- low resilience level/ low tolerance level with others
- panic attacks
- withdrawn/ isolated/ loneliness
- Post-Traumatic Stress disorder
- Secondary Trauma
- Self-Harm/ suicidal thoughts
- 'Feel broken'

The 'cost' to the parent/ carers emotional wellbeing is extensive and includes the economic cost for therapy, GP appointments, prescriptions, support and counselling as well as the associated costs of inability to engage in employment, alongside the impact on others living within the home when the parent/ carer is depressed, anxious or stressed. Living with a parent/ carer who has mental ill health is a recognised Adverse Childhood Experience, in this way there is the indirect cost on other children in the home that can be an indicator for all of the outcomes growing up with adversity points to. The long-term potential for a cycle of emotional and financial 'cost' for families living with CPVA is not unknown, Baker *et al* (2003) asserted '*Over time, a transactional model fit the relationship between parenting stress and behaviour problems: high parenting stress contributed to a worsening in child behaviour problems over time, and high child behaviour problems contributed to a worsening in parenting stress'*. It appears evident therefore, that the real-world costs to families living with CPVA can only be addressed if early intervention is provided, that as yet is not forthcoming, leaving families in the cycle of escalating CPVA behaviours. These escalating behaviours, in turn, increase the emotional cost for the parent/ carer, that then impacts on the economic cost for the family, for example Gordon and Wallace (2015, p.11) specified that parents *'talk about having a level of anger they did not know they possessed and did not demonstrate prior to the child's placement. Often the parents' relationship is in disarray; they may find themselves arguing about the child and about the way to deal with him/her'*. Such discussion highlights how relationship difficulties are inter-related and complex, involving a range of emotions that can then lead to the parents themselves becoming traumatised. The level of trauma parents experience can be life changing and long lasting, as highlighted by Collins (2015 p.22) who stated: '*... I am a traumatised parent. 'I am still coming to terms with those words. It's taken a while for the penny to drop, even though on one level I've known it for some time'*. This statement reiterates and confirms the impact upon parental health if no support is forthcoming when needed and the problems that arise, which can lead to placement breakdown, unemployment, higher risk of divorce or separation and long-term support needed for the family overall and the adults involved individually. Collins (ibid.) continued and outlined the issue of not recognising the real issue, rather simplifying the issue to be something else. For example, he claimed:

> *Much has been written about trauma and its many types and effects. Some of the literature talks about vicarious trauma and how parenting a traumatised child can affect you. As the adoptive parent of a severely damaged young person, who communicates her internal turmoil and hurt through her behaviours, I have learned that living with this trauma changes life dramatically for everyone in the home.* (p.22)

This is not a new claim nor is it different from previous research findings detailing the parental position; yet little as yet appears to have been changed to address this concern for those families living with CPVA on a daily basis, rather there tends to be a *wait and see* approach adopted that continues until such time the family reach crisis. Whether viewed from an economic lens or an emotional lens there is no substance for a *wait and see* approach in supporting families who live with CPVA, insomuch as for most families the longer the wait the higher the costs become.

**Section Summary**

This section provides substantive argument for early intervention as a cost-effective approach to supporting families living with CPVA from both an economic position and a parent/ carer position. The cost of living with CPVA for families is both direct and indirect and falls under two overarching areas- that of economic cost to the family and society, and that of emotional cost to the family and society. The economic costs associated with repair and replacement of items or structural repair, needs to be calculated alongside the economic cost of loss of employment, restricted employment or reduced employment opportunities, that impacts directly onto the household income. Such impact can then lead to the indirect economic position of these families seeking 'state welfare support' via benefit payments. There is also the additional cost of support services for families with reference to policing, health and social care, alongside education, in much the same way as these costs are incurred in any domestic violence relationship. To help address these potential escalating costs early intervention enables these parent/ carers to continue in their employment and to be able to participate in career advancement, should they wish to do so, without restriction. The present position is that the majority of these families find themselves unable to be employed or where they are employed it is either in a reduced capacity or in a restricted capacity. Whilst short term the cost of intervention may seem high, the long-term outcome is cost effective as demonstrated within the 8-family study completed by Wilcox *et al* (2015). In addition to this economic position there is also a substantive cost emotionally for families living with CPVA. The majority of parents (almost 100%) pointed to a direct emotional wellbeing 'cost' for them, as well as a direct 'cost' on their relationships with partners (some families had separated or divorced), siblings within the home (some of whom also engaged in CPVA), wider family members, as well as friends; which led to a feeling of isolation and loneliness for the parent living with CPVA. Such loneliness and related mental wellbeing indicators have been previously outlined by Meredith *et al* (2017) when discussing developmental delay (that was noted by families responding to the CPVA 2018 survey as a diagnosis for their child who engaged in CPVA)

> *It has been well documented that parents of children affected by developmental delays (DD) report considerably more parenting stress than parents of typically*

*developing (TD) children ..The elevated levels of stress experienced by these*
*parents may often be in the clinical range and show a chronic, persistent*
*trajectory which in turn has been linked to adverse outcomes, such as higher levels*
*of maternal distress and depression, poor physical health status, marital*
*difficulties, and reduced overall family wellbeing*

It would therefore be prudent and cost effective to retain the family unit successfully, rather than allow the family unit to struggle or live in 'crisis', given that Kanne and Mazurek (2010) stated *aggressive behaviour is a significant predictor of out of home placements among children and young adults with intellectual disabilities;* a factor also noted by Selwyn *et al* (2014). There are existing policies, legislation and practice indicators to provide the support these families need at a time when they need this support; however, it also appears that this is a rhetorical position and in the real world these families do not benefit from such policies, legislation or practice, a position that requires immediate attention.

# Section 6. Lets Talk About:

# Who supports families living with Child to Parent Violence and Aggression?

One of the main challenges families living with CPVA encounter is seeking appropriate support for the family as a unit, not solely the child displaying CPVA. As discussed within Thorley and Coates (2017c) the family's sense of failure in support provision is not necessarily directed at one service specifically, or one professional group specifically, rather it is the family's experience of being passed from one professional service to another professional service or intervention, the lack of communication and their feelings being undervalued or ignored. It therefore seemed relevant to explore this aspect further within the 2018 CPVA survey and consider which services families had contacted or had received support from, which support services families felt were most effective in their support of the family, which support services families felt were least effective and why they felt this way. Families indicated a range of services they had approached for help as outlined within chart 14:

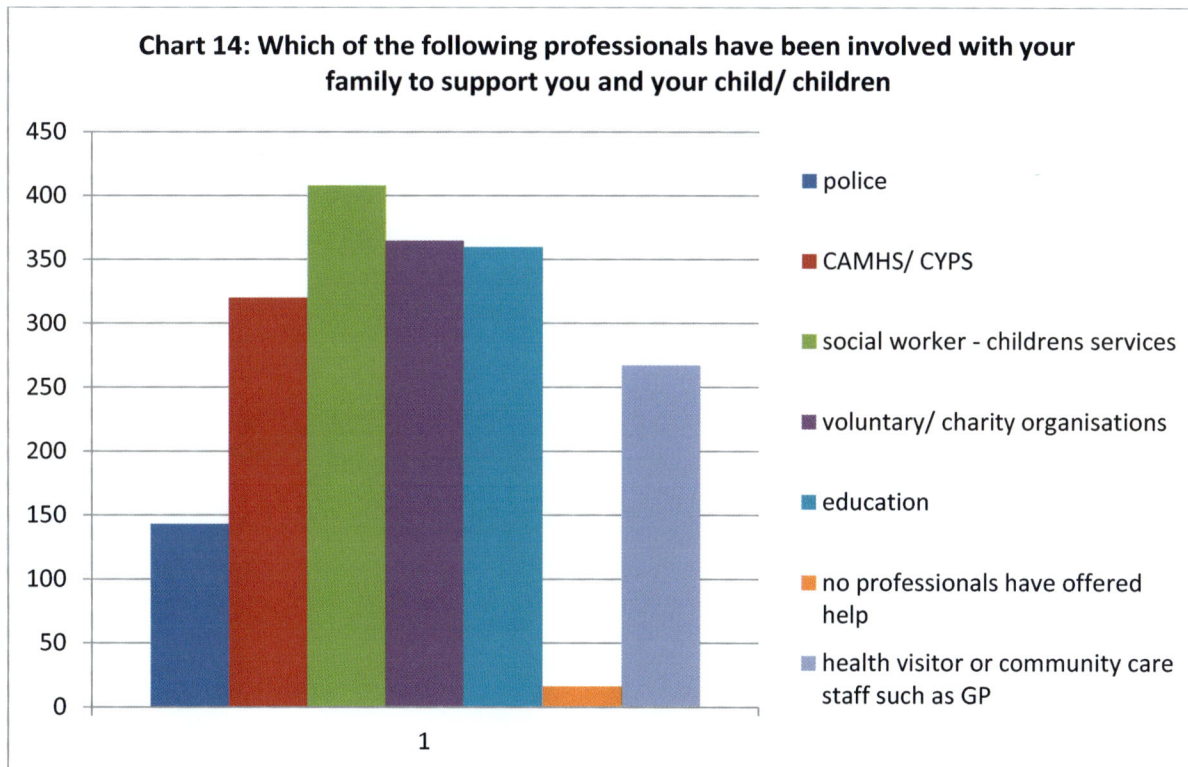

Chart 14: Which of the following professionals have been involved with your family to support you and your child/ children

Legend:
- police
- CAMHS/ CYPS
- social worker - childrens services
- voluntary/ charity organisations
- education
- no professionals have offered help
- health visitor or community care staff such as GP

What is immediately evident within Chart 14 is that families are involved with a myriad of service provision and often with more than one provision simultaneously. This indication demonstrates that the majority of families are receiving support from 4-5 different professional services. Furthermore, more than half of these families receive support or have received support from

- social worker(s) 76%,
- voluntary/ charity support 68%
- education support 67%
- CAMHS/ CYPS 60%
- GP/ Health Visitor 50%
- Police 25%

Such indicators resemble those reported by Thorley and Coates (2017c) where they noted Social Worker support and Education support, featured highly in services involved with the family. Alongside this, the 2018 CPVA survey included responses for support provided by CAMHS/ CYP and compared to previous studies, such as Thorley and Coates (2017c), a higher number of families sought support from CAMHS/ CYPS. Given these indications of multiple service provision for families, it would be anticipated that these families living with CPVA were receiving the support they needed; and that such support provided a co-ordinated wrap around provision, that not only enabled the family to manage their child's behaviour, but also provided them with the knowledge and skills they needed. Providing families with knowledge and skills relating to CPVA empowers the family to be able to provide effective interventions, whilst also reducing the risk of the CPVA behaviour becoming entrenched or escalating; yet such outcomes are not reflected within the real-costs for families living with CPVA as detailed within Section 5. What should not be overlooked is the 3% of families that had been offered no support by any agency or professional, this means these families are isolated and managing alone. Alternatively, it may be these families have not discussed the CPVA behaviour they are living with given the 'hidden' nature of CPVA, however one parent/carer stated that they were *"Told 'no help for families like yours'."* which is highly concerning, particularly when considering another parent/ carers experience who stated:

*No one helped for about seven years, then everyone got involved, but no one actually did anything to help. We just went round in circles from agency to agency, police to GP to CAMHs to hospital to social services to education, back to charity/voluntary agency, the police, GP, CAMHS etc. This happened repeated for years and years. They were so proud of the inter-agency approach, but we got no actual help. Then I threatened to kill child and myself and then we got specialist provision. The police were the most help as they got to know child really well and offered most support to child and myself. It was like the police were acting as social workers.*

What this underscore's is the disparity between support provision and the real cost indicated by families, pointing to lack of support. It is therefore apparent that being provided with support, and being supported by providers, are different entities from the parent position. For this reason, specific questions were included to expand parent/ carer views of professional involvement and support available to them as follows:

- *If professionals were previously involved- who do you feel were the most supportive and effective- please briefly add how/ why* (eliciting 448 responses)
- *If professionals were previously involved- who do you feel were the least supportive and effective- please briefly add how/ why* (eliciting 448 responses)
- *Do you currently have professional support for your family- if so who provides this and how*

The responses from parent/ carers tended to fall into 3 distinct areas: Voluntary Agency/ Charity Agency provision, Statutory Service provision or privately funded. Further subcategories could then be ascertained as follows:

| Voluntary/ Charitable | Private | Statutory Provision |
|---|---|---|
| Adoption related | Counselling | Police |
| SEND specific | Psychologist | Health: Community general |
| 'Other' | Specialised Therapist | Health: CAMHS/ CYPS |
| | | Education (School) |
| | | Children's Services: social worker |
| | | Children's Services: specialist social worker |

To clarify how families viewed the support they receive, or have received, alongside which services appear to be most effective according to the families in receipt of this support, the responses were considered individually and then collectively, for each of the sub-groups outlined. Whilst these responses and feelings reported by parent/ carers are by nature biased and based on personal opinion, they are not of any lesser value than that of the professional when presenting their opinion. Whilst professional opinion has not been included in this particular study, that set out to discover how families feel and how they and their family were impacted upon when living with CPVA, further studies should not discount including professionals, the merging of both opinions can be enlightening in developing and informing service provision, what support is needed by families and how this support should be provided. Within the responses from parent/ carers regarding who they found to be most and least supportive or effective in providing help for the family, it was interesting to note that only 2 parent/ carers pointed to a voluntary service provision as being least effective or supportive, compared to opinion of Statutory Service provision every respondent included at least one Statutory Service as least effective and least supportive. These parent/ carers felt that the Statutory Service had not only failed to help them when they requested help but had also failed their child and any other children in the home environment.

Voluntary/ Charity service provision featured most frequently as 'most effective' previously and 'most effective' currently. Within the parent/carer responses 365 parent/ carers included Voluntary or charitable organisations, of these parent/ carers 280 noted the provision as 'most effective' for their family's needs. Such findings do not suggest that the remaining provision was ineffective rather it may be that another provision was more so; although 2 parent/ carers did include charitable organisations within their 'least' responsive and least effective professionals involved with the family. This is important if cost effective interventions are to be provided as a process of 'wrap around' support for families, in that those services families feel are the most supportive and effective are the ones that need to be developed to meet the need of all families living with CPVA. Participants noted several ways in which Voluntary/ Charity services had supported them and hence why they noted them as most effective or supportive of their family, this included those funded via Adoption Support Funding (ASF) for example:

- *Therapeutic intervention via asf*
- *LACES were the first to take us seriously.*
- *We found Adoption UK very helpful. They run brilliant courses at affordable prices.*
- *My social worker though Adoption matters, Also an adopter*
- *Ddp therapist/ therapeutic life story work practitioner funded through ASF*
- *Voluntary organisations and child psychologist.*
- *Volunteer from Barbados only one to offer weekly outing*
- *Oldest's independent psychotherapist (based with large adoption support agency) who is experienced in adoption, trauma and attachment, and youngest's independent play*

*therapist with similar experience; oldest's school. They listen, understand, do not blame or judge, can suggest effective strategies grounded in PACE, NVR, TP, DDP. They appreciate how hard and frightening it can be and can keep us all in mind.*
- *My social worker, who works for Barnardo's.*
- *Private therapy sessions funded via ASF - voluntary self help youth club*
- *Voluntary organisations / charities - far less judgemental, able to see the big picture rather than just focus on one aspect eg health or child protection or education.*

Alongside voluntary and charitable services, that sit outside of Statutory provision, are privately funded professionals, within responses received 56 families (more than 10% of participating parent/ carers) had engaged privately funded support and recorded this as 'most effective' or 'most supportive' for their family noting:

- *My own psychotherapist who I was seeing before adoption has been most valuable support…*
- *We got a private diagnosis which was most helpful. NHS and school/social support have been non existent….*
- *Private psychologist. Autism outreach team….*
- *Private therapist but other professionals unwilling to accept her recommendations.*

Such indicators highlight that families begin to 'lose faith' in the provision available to them as a Statutory service. This is not unknown, previous studies such as Adfam and Against Violence and Abuse (2012), Selwyn et al (2014), Thorley and Coates (2017c), Adoption UK (2018) and Hollins (2017) all noted similar responses from families. Outside of the privately funded, or voluntary/ charity support, there are mixed responses relating to statutory providers. Some families felt these were beneficial whilst the majority did not find these helpful and often felt they were being labelled as 'poor parents'. To reflect upon why Statutory Service is viewed from such differential positions parent/ carer voices need to be heard; irrespective of whether this is the parents own 'biased' view. Parent Carer positions need to take precedence when building support and/ or intervention approaches for families living with CPVA; one that is embedded in good relationships founded on respect for the parent/ carer, rather than the current status quo that continues to point to a real post-code lottery of support.

If CPVA is viewed as a form of domestic violence then it would be anticipated families could be supported by the Police. Similar to the findings in 2017 (Thorley and Coates 2017c), the Police tended to be viewed positively overall. Within the responses to who previously or currently supported the family, 143 parent/ carers noted the Police; of which 100 parent/ carers included the police as 'the most supportive/ effective' to them as a family. This provides further argument for reconsidering Child Safety Orders (outlined in Section 3) and how these are applied, to enable a more pro-active role for the Police in helping families, prior to the escalation and entrenchment of the behaviour occurring; given that one year on from the 2017 CPVA survey it continues to be Policing that appear to provide the support these families need. It is feasible to suggest that the Police are most effective due to their position in understanding and dealing with 'violence' in the home; insomuch as the Police, by nature of their occupation, are involved in a number of domestic violence concerns and therefore may hold more experience than perhaps a Health Visiting, Teaching or Post Adoption Social work, as a service provision in working with families who live with domestic violence; such positions are supported within parent/carer responses that state, for example:

- *"Police were very understanding"* -
- *"The police have been the most supportive but we only encounter them when the violence is extreme."* -
- *"Police called once, responded quickly and were sympathetic"* -
- *"Police useful during actual incidents - calm and non-judgemental."* -
- *"Police were most supportive, compassionate, non judgemental and resourceful"*.

Whilst the majority of police provision was seen to be effective and supportive by 70% of parent/ carers, 7% of parent/ carers disagreed and noted the Police as one of the least helpful or supportive professionals they had contacted. However, it should be noted that these parent/ carers went onto explain the reason the Police were least effective was due to the age of the child engaging in CPVA (under 10 years of age) rather than other issues. One parent/carer did note that they felt the Police were judging them and that they were 'poor parents' for 'criminalising' their child's behaviour, whilst this may only be one parent/ carer's view such responses towards families are unhelpful and encourage families to continue to remain 'hidden'.

In contrast to the Police service, Children's Services received far more mixed reactions and comments relating to how effective they were as a Statutory Service provision in supporting families living with CPVA. Overall, 408 parent/ carers were in contact with Children's Services but only 60 parent/carer's included Children's Services as being 'most effective and supportive' of their family and where this was noted it tended to be within more specialist service provision such as Post Adoption Support or Disability support services, as detailed within:

- *Post adoption support have visited & supported regularly & made lots of referrals eg CAMHS*
- *Post Adoption Support SW as she has offered help, support & sources therapy which has worked*
- *SPAB (was previously the Inclusion Team) our family support worker is excellent*
- *Disabiliry social worker so helpful in accessing personal budget and pressuring schools/Camhs/la to support*
- *Our own fostering Support Worker was very supportive, the Local Authority Social Worker really couldn't care less.*
- *The social worker from the Child in Need team, when I reported my child as a CIN because we were getting no help from any professionals, they came in, took control and gave everyone responsibilities*

Of greater concern is the notable number of families who felt their social worker was not effective, not understanding or not supportive, so much so replies included: *"Our post adoption social worker barely sees us"*. Of the 408 parent/ carers living with CPVA who included Children's Services as a professional involved with the family either previously or currently, 348 included this service within their response for least supportive and least effective. Dissatisfaction with Children's Services included comments of lack of appreciation of the issues, or repositioning the behaviour as an anticipated 'normative' developmental phase, therefore discounting parent/ carer concerns as unfounded, for example:

- *Social workers. Totally minimize CPV as "normal childhood behaviour". Seem unaware of issues around control related to early life trauma and the implications for family life*
- *Social Work asked what we had done beforehand and blamed us - never discussed with child suggested if we colour in together for 15 mins per day situation would not escalate!*
- *all blamed my parenting, refused to listen, refused to think outside their training*
- *Social services child protection teams - look to blame parents and poor parenting*
- *LA made severe mistakes when making decisions about her care causing more unnecessary trauma*
- *Social workers incredibly judgemental, uninformed, unhelpful, undermining, abusive and appeared to have an agenda unrelated to the needs of our family or the reality of what we were living with.*
- *just 'she is testing you so must feel safe' type platitudes.*
- *Social service have no idea about CPV or FASD and only focus on parenting, so no understanding when their techniques have no effect*
- *Some of the social workers were so inexperienced they were of no use*
- *Social services disability team, suggested visual timetable, no help 'unless you dump him on our doorstep'*

This suggests there is an urgent need to ensure all social workers employed within Children and Family services require training as a matter of urgency in supporting families who live with CPVA. Social workers are required by Law to engage with families of children who have disabilities, as well as those children who are Looked After or have been Previously Looked After, highlighting the necessity for all of these professionals to be updated in their knowledge, skills and competencies if they are to be effective in their role., and whilst case loading is cited is the main concern in Social Work at this time, it appears from the 'case' position that it is lack of knowledge, understanding or skill in being effective in the role undertaken that creates the difficulties. For many parent/carers there was a feeling that as long as everything went to plan then they received the support they anticipated, but if things were not as per the expected norm social workers struggled. There was particular concern over newly qualified social workers or those with minimal experience and their lack of understanding for more complex children and the needs of those children.

Education is a further Statutory Service provision that is designed to meet the learning and developmental needs of children and young people across the United Kingdom. Children legally have to attend school from aged 5 years to 16 years and onto 18 years if they do not enter employment training opportunities whilst Local Authorities have a Statutory obligation to provide educational places for children to attend[40]. For this reason, there is a need for teachers and school staff to recognise the impact of living with domestic violence (as one of the acknowledged Adverse Childhood Experience Indicators) as an impact not only for families but for any sibling within the household. Much in the same manner in which the experience of children with SEND is variable across the scale of very good to very poor, the response by schools to children who engage in CPVA is also variable across the range. Within responses received, 360 parent/ carers included Education staff as professionals they were or had been involved with; of these only 60 parent/ carers included school staff in their 'most effective/ supportive' reply. As seen in Children's Services, it was those staff within specialist school provision, such as the SENCo and Pastoral Support Team, that were noted as being most effective and supportive to families, for example:

- *The children's school, which is a school for special need , where they support and understand my children's needs and ours as a family.*
- *School, especially head and SENCO*
- *The children's school, which is a school for special need , where they support and understand my children's needs and ours as a family. Also, the SENCO at their previous mainstream schools who supported me with their EHCP'S.*
- *School - arranged a meeting with outreach services*

---

[40] At the time of writing it is notable that very many children, particularly those who are Looked After, those who have Previously been Looked After and those who have SEND are without provision contrary to the requirements set out for Local Authorities.

- *Education. The school have been supportive and tried to find strategies to help him attend … They also re-referred to CAMHS for us and communicated with social work. The most important thing they've done is not put pressure on us to stick to a timetable and allowed great deal of flexibility as well as being calm, empathic and supportive. They are solution focused and listen and learn from our strategies.*

Part of the difficulty for parent/ carers in gaining support from the school reflected where the child attended, of the 300 parent/ carers who pointed to schools being least effective and supportive, 75% of these children attended a mainstream setting. It is well documented in current media and organisational publications that the current Educational system for children who are Looked After, have been Previously Looked After or are SEND are significantly disadvantaged within the framework for education provision and as such are more likely to be excluded for behaviour issues, more likely to be 'off-rolled' as an informal exclusion and are more likely to be left at home without any education provision for periods up to one year or more. Whilst it is not the purpose of this report to detail all of the educational issues children who engage in CPVA encounter, it supports the views of parents that this provision is neither effective or supportive for parent/ carers, their children and their family. Such dissatisfaction can be seen in parent// carer responses including:

- *Education- as they failed to believe the issues and safety issues at home*
- *Teachers Not trained in SEND*
- *Education caused first child's anxieties to increase which in turn impacted hugely on all our family*
- *Education because they only addressed the behaviour with no support or understanding or intention to look for the reason, dealing with any issue with punishment which further exacerbated the situation*
- *Education at primary school support varied and one HT was completely unsupportive. High school for second child, support has not been there. In general schools have ignored the needs of adopted children and any additional diagnoses.*
- *Schools, they don't understand.*
- *Education … did nothing to help.*
- *Special school staff were appalling and abandoned us all after saying they couldn't meet our needs*
- *Education - inconsistent, not knowledgeable about trauma and attachment, at times inflexible in their approach*
- *Senco & headteacher at mainstream schools*
- *School …- try to fob you off and minimise concerns or presume issues are related to parenting (despite having another child patented the same way and not having aggression as an issue and parent having both an education, child development and Child health professional background). Complete lack of support.*
- *Head of primary school saw child two as a discipline problem, had no understanding of underlying communication problem and only realised / acknowledged in the last year how bullying by mainstream kids impacted on my child. Many teachers and management in comprehensive also didn't have the understanding, skills,*

> *resourcefulness or resilience to deal with a multitude of behaviour. We found ourselves playing the SEN card to prevent our child being excluded.*
> - *Education- daughters first school failed to cope and deliberately made matters much worse*
> - *Education made me feel incompetent as a parent and as if i was lying about her needs*

It is evident within these responses that parents have little faith in the ability for schools to provide fair and equal access for all children, similar to that found within the Lamb Inquiry (2009) and whilst the Lamb Inquiry that did not seek to investigate CPVA as such, it did highlight the inconsistencies and lack of support for parents of children with SEND, following which little appears to have changed. This is particularly relevant given the relationship between the risk of CPVA occurring and those children with SEND behaviour related conditions, outlined within DSM-V (Section 4). With heightened risk of CPVA occurrence noted within those children who have diagnosed behavioural difficulties, as well as those children who have experienced loss and trauma, or are living with attachment difficulties, there may be an anticipation that families are able to seek support and help from Health Providers. Parent/ carers responded to indicate that 320 parent/ carers had received or were currently receiving support from Child and Adolescence Mental Health services (CAMHS) of which only 10% felt this provision was effective and supportive. This means that 90% of families felt the provision was least effective and supportive, yet with reference to the indicators in Section 4, outlining the relationship between CPVA and DSM-V conditions, it would be anticipated that CAMHS should be one of the most effective and supportive provisions for families. Parents disagree and state that: *"CAMHS had no understanding of the needs of adopted children (child 2)"* ... *"CAMHS showed no willingness to help"* .... *"CAMH impossibly slow in helping"*. Reasons for parent/ carers including CAMHS as the least effective and supportive professional help they had received included lengthy delays, little appreciation of the real issue and not listening to parent/ carer for example:

- *Camhs refusal to access x 2, 5 yrs later now waiting 2 yr minimum on waiting list.*
- *CAMHS - still on waiting list 16 months after initial assessment (for which there was a previous waiting list of several months)*
- *We were told by CAMHS he 'wasn't disabled enough'*
- *camhs as they didn't explore the reasons behind the behaviour*
- *CAMHS particularly. Dreadful. Unhelpful and judgemental*
- *CAMHS very rigid in that can offer what they have, regardless of its appropriate-ness to the need. CAMHS also judgemental, unhelpful, superior, unwilling to listen*
- *Mainstream CAMHS - no understanding of adoption*
- *Camhs - only medication offered*

- *Camhs took 4 years of talking to have a 1hr chat with child psychologist who identified cause and a book we could learn from*
- *CAMHS and Social Care have been very unsupportive and have several times told us to grow up*
- *Camhs. Dismissive. not offering help. Unprofessional re-diagnosing. Not listening*
- *Camhs just gave parenting advice around consequence and reward. Strategies that do not work.*
- *Camhs-under camhs for 2 years. Took 1.5yrs for diagnosis to be issued. No strategies given to us just advised of local autism website.*

CAMHS is provided as part of the National Health Service provision with a requirement to help support those with mental health needs. What is highlighted by this lack of provision and lack of service is the multiple family members that are being overlooked. Within families where CPVA occurs there are all of the following members who require support for their mental wellbeing:

- The child displaying CPVA
- Siblings and other children in the house who are living with domestic abuse
- Parents/ carers who are at high risk of depression, anxiety and secondary trauma
- Any other adults living in the home

It can therefore be suggested that at present CAMHS overall appears to have little understanding or appreciation of the nature of CPVA and how this impacts across the entire family, not solely the child who engages in CPVA. Both in economic costs and emotional costs, it is far more effective and supportive to provide the help these families require at the outset, rather than wait until such time the entire family unit require support from CAMHS and Adult Mental Health Services, as the behaviour escalates and become entrenched. Whilst debate may arise about the nature of using DSM-V diagnosis within the UK, that may foster opinion away from recognising Intermittent Explosive Disorder, similar to debate around Attention Deficit Hyperactivity Disorder, there is a clear definition within the World Health Organisation Classification of Diseases that also highlights CPVA as a conduct disorder and therefore recognition should be given to CPVA in its own right. Whilst further debate seeks to position CPVA within the behaviour traits of 'other' childhood conduct disorders such as

- Autistic Spectrum Disorder,
- Foetal Alcohol Syndrome,
- Attention Deficit Hyperactivity Disorder,
- Post-Traumatic Stress Disorder,

- Anxiety,
- Developmental Delay,

this merely masks issues families are living with, by placing CPVA into a wide range of conduct disorders, as an atypical behaviour trait across the range of disorders, rather than recognising CPVA as a co-morbidity. Recognising CPVA as a conduct disorder specifically is allowing for CPVA to be identified, named and recognised as a co-morbid condition; in much the same way as Depression can coincide with Anxiety, Post-traumatic Stress can coincide with depression and/or anxiety and autism can coincide with Learning Difficulties, all as co-morbid conditions. Fundamental to accepting CPVA as a co-morbid conduct disorder acknowledges World Health Organisation classifications to be applied in full and places CPVA within *Conduct disorders confined to family contexts*. Accepting this co-morbity then acknowledges previous argument, that CPVA is frequently found to be displayed by children have a diagnosed conduct disorder, a factor found not only in the 2018 CPVA survey but one previously reported for example:

> *Data from Parentline shows that families calling about aggression in children are more likely to report that their children are not enjoying good mental health and wellbeing. Many appear to be displaying behaviours associated with conduct disorders and a number of families are already in contact with specialist Child and Adolescent Mental Health Services (CAMHS). Conduct disorders are the most common childhood psychiatric disorders* (Family Lives, 2011 p.4) (my emphaisis)

Following studies also pointed to conduct disorders including: Anderson (2011), Calvete *et* al (2012), Contrares and Cano (2016), Thorley and Coates (2017), Adoption UK (2018). Such indicators point to the basis of much CPVA displayed is embedded within conduct disorders, and as such cannot therefore be considered as CPVA within the global definition for this behaviour; rather there appears to be two distinct categories of CPVA that are displayed by children:

1st: that of intention, whereby the current definition and procedures do reflect intervention for such behaviour via Policing and Home office (2015) Guidance.

2nd: that which is not intentional and is a conduct disorder, that is not currently recognised or addressed in Health provision at this time, leading by default for this to be supported via the 'intention' category of support

Alongside CAMHS, the NHS also provides community support via the General Practitioner (GP) and Health Visitor as well as the School Nurse team for children and young people. Within health provision collectively, GPs featured most as supportive and effective, in that 267 parent/ carers included the GP or Primary Health provision previously or currently and 125 of these parent/carers responses included their GP or Health provider as 'most effective/ supportive'. This suggests that 47% of families were happy with the support their GP or Primary Health team provided. Whilst this indicates that further development continues to be required, GPs are significantly more effective and supportive than their counterparts within Health, Childrens Services or Education. Parent/ carers stated that it was the *"GP as he recognised there was a real reason for the behaviour and fully supported us"* and *"The most supportive people have been the School nurse and my GP without them no one else has listened or bothered"*. Such indicators contrast sharply with that for CAMHS another Statutory Health service provision. Conversely, to those parent/ carers who were satisfied with the support their Primary Health team provided 24% were unhappy with the support and intervention provided, they claimed:

- *GP…. felt passed on from one agency to the next, no impact at all other than frustration*
- *Local GP- no help at all*
- *Gp....didnt act for over a year. Felt like i wasnt believed*

Appreciation for and understanding of the impact for families when living with CPVA and relying upon a post-code lottery for any help to be forthcoming, enables the cost of living with CPVA outlined in Section 4 to be fully appreciated. It therefore seems apparent that if any change is to occur, it needs to start with dissemination of what living with CPVA means for families, the provision of a holistic wrap around service for all family members and to recognise the parent position without prejudice and bias impacting on professional action.

Irrespective of Statutory service provision one theme continually emerged for dissatisfaction with effectiveness and support from Education, Children's Services and Health (both CAMHS and Primary Care) that parent/ carers indicated. Parents/ carers repeatedly pointed to a lack of understanding of SEND, Trauma and Attachment difficulties, by those responsible for providing support to them, so that they felt that what was provided was neither supportive of effective. Such lack of training and understanding in SEND is a known indicator for teachers within England at this time, with suggestions of including SEND into core Teacher Training, as well as including Learning difficulties within core training for medical professionals. Whilst such development may increase awareness of the condition the child has, it may not improve the support parent/ carers receive; as this is a personal relationship between professional and parent/ carer built on trust and empathy. What continues to be evident within the data generated is that despite more discussion regarding CPVA since Thorley and Coates (2017) reported on this, and all of the ensuing and previous discussions, documentaries and podcasts/ broadcasts, there is very much a status quo position for families. This is evident within the data generated for the 2018 CPVA survey that continues to point to families who seek support from multiple contacts and yet still feel the support received was not helpful. Given the duration between the 2017 CPVA survey and the 2018 CPVA survey it is reasonable to argue that there has been insufficient time to develop understanding or interventions that help families living with CPVA, what must be remembered is that CPVA has been discussed for more than four decades yet the status quo remains, as illustrated within chart 15:

**Chart 15: In your own experience do you feel ... are better informed now and more understanding than they were 18 months ago**

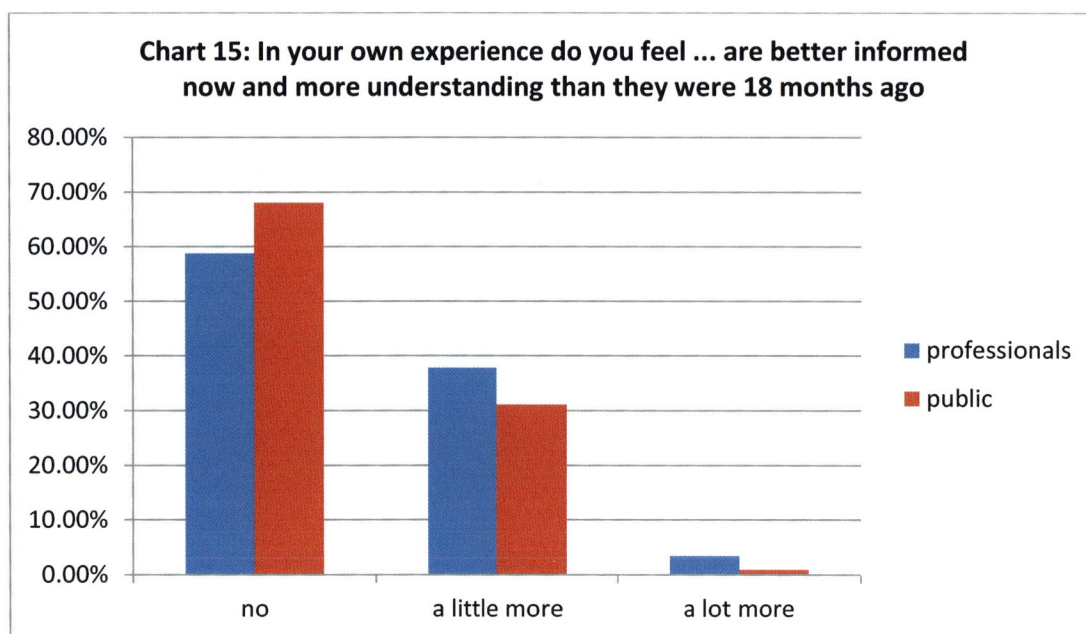

There is recognition of a slight movement in the understanding of Professionals according to parent/ carers who live with CPVA but not sufficiently so to enable them to now receive the support and intervention they desperately require. It is also important to recognise that whilst seeking support from one service provision may be unhelpful due to lack of understanding for parent/ carers and their families, the data continues to point to a collective lack of appreciation by a range of providers in supporting families living with CPVA. This then leads to families feeling isolated as previously detailed within Thorley and Coates (2017b) or having little choice, as indicated by Selwyn et al (2014) and outlined within Section 3 and 4, to reduce the enormous influencing and consequential impact living with CPVA can have on the families'

overall wellbeing. Recognising that these families do seek support from a range of services, it is disturbing to acknowledge that the status quo continues and that they continue to contact more than one service for support without support forthcoming. One of the reasons this may occur is how such responses are made and the position of the professional contacted, the professionals knowledge of CPVA as a concern in itself, as well as the legal position they hold, as professionals overall, for protecting children or adults. How professionals and support organisations view CPVA is very much dependent upon the lens they 'see' CPVA through as previously argued by Bonnick (2017). Using their professional 'lens' to view the family enables prejudice and bias to unfold, if such a view is only informed by what the professional currently knows without recognising they, the professional, may have knowledge 'gaps' or limitations in their ability to provide support, for example whilst the Police may recognise CPVA is a concern for families and includes children under the age of 10 years; the current legal position encourages families to feel a police intervention is not available. Moreover, if the option is to view CVPA under Legal argument as domestic abuse and 'charge' adolescents accordingly with an 'unlawful act' this too can become a barrier to seeking support; as noted by Family Lives (2011 p.2) when updating their 2010 report.

Family Lives reported that 20% (1:5) of families didn't seek any form of help or support due to what they perceived to be the lasting impact on their child's life chances, and rather than seek support these families continued in silence hoping to manage the child's behaviour. Such suggestions need to be employed in educating professionals about CPVA specifically and the wider impact for all family members to enable parent/ carers to seek the help they need. Outside of the legal position, those professionals from Health (including Primary Care Professionals), Childrens Services (Including Social care) and Education (including Teachers and School staff) that determine CPVA as a behaviour concern employing labels such as 'challenging Behaviour, EBD (Emotional Behaviour Difficulties), ADHD (Attention deficit Hyperactivity Disorder), ASD (Autistic Spectrum Disorder) ODD (Oppositional Defiant Disorder) or CD (Conduct Disorder) limit their view on the impact of CPVA for families, by focusing on the diagnosis rather than the situation families find themselves in; and looking only at the behaviour in terms of a single diagnosis rather than as a co-morbidity and a condition classified as a conduct disorder with or without co-morbidity. In this way using diagnostic labels can be unhelpful for families unless CPVA is recognised as a co-morbidity alongside other named conduct disorders, recognising that CPVA requires specific and targeted support and intervention. The limitation that such labelling has is shown in parent/ carers responses to how effective and supportive Statutory Service provision has been, in that they state:

> "CBT is useless a complete waste of time its not that he knows when he is doing this so he can't control his behaviour that's why CBT didn't work, they were telling him its about changing his behaviour and the choices he makes but he doesn't intend to behave like this then we were discharged and now have to go and wait again".

In addition, parent/ carers also felt that whilst PACE[41] and NVR[42] helped some families, it did not help all parents. The main problems appear to be based in assumption, that reflects a one size fits all approach rather than the individualised need of the child. For some parent/ carers NVR had offered them the resolution they were seeking and helped them to feel in control again, for others it did not have the desired impact. In contrast to the legal framework available to the Police from the Home Office (2015), when families report CPVA the NHS professionals, Childrens Services and Education do not have a universal policy or practice indicators in place; this leaves it very much up to individual professionals how they respond and leads to the variations noted within the responses by parent/ carers. Such variations were outlined by Holt and Retford (2013) in their study of practitioner responses, whereby socially unacceptable child behaviour was noted as the only policy one practitioner could associate with for the CPVA displayed. This form of response may not be helpful to parents and can, in some instances, exacerbate the problems families are attempting to find support for; as noted by Wilcox *et al* (2015). Wilcox *et al* (2015) acknowledged the levels of support were difficult reflecting the lack of policy guidance for professionals working with children and families, along with variable levels of co-ordination on CPVA. Furthermore, they agreed that support was inconsistent as a consequence of differential levels of professional skills, knowledge, and competencies in this specific area of need. Developing a good practice protocol that all professionals can refer to would be beneficial to all families living with CPVA, insomuch as they would then know what to expect and who to approach for help, rather than the random trial selection process they currently engage in. Developing a universal protocol would also prevent children being placed into unhelpful alternative categories including becoming a 'behaviour' concerns or behaviour difficulty or anti-social.

---

[41] Pace parenting programme: playfulness, acceptance, curiosity and empathy. Developed by Dan Hughes, for full details of this approach see: https://ddpnetwork.org/about-ddp/meant-pace/
[42] Non Violent Resistance – see Coogan D and Lauster E (2015) Non Violent Resistance Programme Handbook for Practitioners – Responding to Child to Parent Violence in Practice

**Section Summary**

It is evident from the responses that these parents participating within the 2018 CPVA survey have made attempts to access support without success. Whilst some support has been good, much has not. In part this is created by the vagueness surrounding CPVA by professionals involved. To support families effectively and efficiently all professionals irrespective of background need to understand what CPVA is. There is a wide held definition currently employed that determines all CPVA to be intentional, yet the majority of parents within research to date and within this study, argue this does not apply to their child or their family or their reality. As outlined within section four categorising CPVA as a Conduct Disorder as provided by DSM-V and ICD-10/ ICD-11 is the foundation for developing a service that meets the needs of both the child engaging in CPVA and family living with CPVA. Exploring why this has not occurred over the past four decades, when CPVA was first identified, is in part due to the updating of DSM-V and ICD-10 (ICD-11) in recognising this behaviour, as well as professional awareness of Conduct Disorders, to enable them to include those applicable; whilst there is disagreement about applying all of the DSM-V categories within the UK due to their American origins, recognising potential indicators such as Oppositional Defiance Disorder, a condition in the early years that can continue, allows these families to be supported, this is further demonstrated if *Intermittent Explosive Behaviour*, as discussed within section four, is acknowledged as the underlying yet often overlooked, explanation for the conundrum that is CPVA without 'intent'. This section highlights that despite four decades of research reporting, there continues to be a myriad of responses from professionals to parent/ carers, when they seek help and support for their child who is engaging in CPVA, themselves as parent and for members of the family living within the same household. Furthermore, the majority of effective support and interventions are provided by the voluntary/ charity sector rather than Statutorily provision, or has been privately funded by families. This raises concerns about how statutory service professionals engage with families seeking help; and why the least support and least effective interventions are those the Statutory Service professionals provide overall. It is apparent across this section and that of section five, both in terms of an economic argument and an emotional argument, professionals need to receive training in ICD-10 (ICD-11) F.91-0 *Conduct disorder confined to family context* and related categories, to enable these professionals to address CPVA concerns raised by families. There is also an urgent need to consider why DSM-V/ ICD-10 (ICD-11) categories have not been explored in full previously, to recognise CPVA as a conduct disorder;

for example, as Intermittent Explosive Behaviour. Recognising CPVA as a Conduct Disorder then enables CPVA to be a co-morbid diagnosis rather than a facet of something else, that in turn can reduce the perceived impact CPVA has on families lives by professionals. Allowing CPVA to be independently recognised as a co-morbidity also enables all underpinning policies and legislation regarding SEND to be applied; and accepts not all children with an alternative Conduct Disorder or behavioural condition will engage in CPVA, but some might. In this way it is accepted that CPVA can coincide or develop later, alongside other behavioural conditions; including Attention Deficit Hyperactivity Disorder, Autistic Spectrum Disorder, Foetal Alcohol Syndrome, Post Traumatic Stress Disorder and aligned Neurological conditions, but that CPVA is not a facet of these conditions. There is an urgent need to ensure all Social Workers and Mental Health professionals engaging with Children and Families are trained in CPVA and able to support those children and families they work with. More importantly there is a need to recognise that CPVA can be perceived by professionals via their own professional 'lens', a lens that can add bias, misunderstanding, prejudice and presumption about the child, the parent/carer and the family. Proposals set out for recognising CPVA within established DSM-V and ICD-10 (ICD-11) indicators suggested within section four are upheld within this section, highlighting further why there is a fundamental change required in how these families are perceived; and how these families are supported. The first step in removing barriers for families is to recognise CPVA behaviour as ICD-10 (ICD-11) F.91-0 *Conduct disorder confined to family context* (World Health Organisation, 2018) and not presume to label such behaviour under another condition, thereby masking and occluding the real issue. Without updated knowledge, skills and competencies alongside the development of a universal policy all professionals can follow there will be no change in the status quo for families seeking help and support.

# Section 7: Lets Talk About:

# What would families living with CPVA suggest happens next?

Although the notion and discussion of CPVA has been reported for more than four decades, those families who live with CPVA do not feel that much has changed. Irrespective of the good will or good intentions of those undertaking research into this area, proposals of what needs to happen next and indicators of good practice suggests little has altered in the real world for these families; as detailed across sections 2, 3, 4, 5 and 6. In part, this seems to reflect the focus that has been placed on CPVA studies to date as either:

- An adolescent concern
- A concern for Adopters only
- Related to children that were Looked After or Previously Looked After only
- A 'Poor Parenting' concern

Such identifiers lead to support being provided under the 'category' rather than support being provided to meet the child, the parent/ carer and the family's needs individually and specifically. More concerningly this overlooks very many families living with children who have SEND and display CPVA, due to the child or family not 'fitting' into the above classifications, for example birth families, irrespective of whether or not they are couple households or single parent households, and birth parents of children who have SEND. It is therefore important to recognise the experiences of these families and consider what they suggest should happen next. Generating information from parent/carers living with CPVA recognises that in terms of their child and their family, these parent/ carers are equally experienced and equally knowledgeable about what works, what helps and what is needed, to effectively support them and their family. Within the survey parent/ carers were asked for their opinion, and whilst this may arguably produce biased or prejudiced data; without this opinion, based on their lived-in experiences, any future proposals may miss the real needs these parents have. To consider in more depth how families may be supported more effectively the following questions were included into the 2018 survey:

1. Since the initial survey in Dec 2016 there has been a lot more media attention and social media discussion around child to parent aggression/ violence - do you feel this has been helpful – why

2.  What is the one main thing you would like to see changed in supporting families like yours with their children
3.  Have you been offered any training to help you manage your child's behaviour
4.  Helping Professionals to support families: what would be the main thing you would include about child to parent aggression or violence in a good practice guide for professionals
5.  Helping Families: what would be the main thing you would include about child to parent aggression or violence in a good practice guide for families

Responses were varied and offered an insight into how families can be supported alongside what has been offered to date. On reflecting over the period between December 2016 and when these parent/ carers completed their responses suggests that the media attention and social media discussions have been helpful for some (66%) whilst creating further problems for others, increasing the stress and impact they already live with (34%). For those parent/ carers, two-thirds of those participating, the media attention had been helpful for two distinct reasons that were included in their response, that they *'felt less alone'* and that they were *'not the only one';* this in itself is the most effective support social media and media coverage could provide, in helping these parents to feel less *'blamed'.* This has enabled these parent/ carers to discuss their experience more readily with wider family and friends and begin to *'uncover'* their lived-in experiences that was previously *'hidden'.* However, for the remaining one-third of parent/ carers, who disagreed and did not feel it helped or had not seen any media coverage, so felt they could not comment, valid argument was offered including:

- *To be honest, I haven't really liked it. I think the media want exciting stories which make out children to be monsters. I suspect that's contributed to my family's rejection of my children.*
- *Not helpful as still very unrecognised and seldom discussed due to stigma, other people's attitudes can be very dismissive.*

Furthermore, they felt that across society overall there was heightened *'Blame parents'* approach adopted by not only professionals but more readily society overall. These parent/ carers also pointed to how social media had led to far more members of society, qualified or not, offering advice and guidance of how best to address CPVA so that *everyone's an expert* further limiting these parents being listened too. Such discussion also highlighted that due to how media portray children who engage in CPVA, without real reflection of the child's individual needs, encourages *limited viewpoints* that result in limited solutions be this support, interventions or strategies. As reflected within responses and detailed in Chart 16, the majority of parent/ carers had not been offered training to date, to help them manage their child's needs.

**Chart 16: have you been offered training**

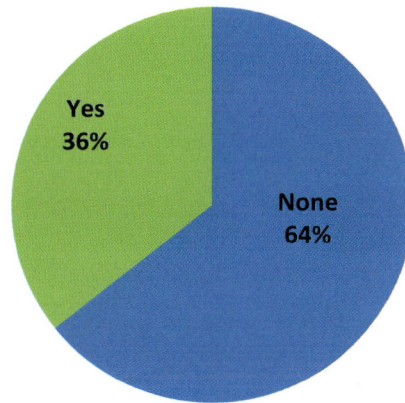

Yes
36%

None
64%

More detailed analysis of the training provided to the minority of parents suggests whilst not forthcoming, those parents who are adopters are more likely to access training than those who are not, for example kinship carers and birth parents. This is in part due to funding, as those parents who are adopters are able to access funding through the Adoption Support Fund towards interventions for their children (as are SGOs) however such funding is not available to any other parent group including Kinship carers or birth parents. However, families who are not adopters do engage with other sources of support as noted within Section 6. For the 192 parent/carers who had received training, training offered was in three main avenues

**Chart 17: training offered to parent/ carers**

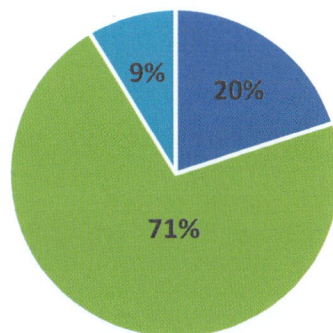

9%

20%

71%

■ Positive Parenting Programme/ Course ■ NVR course or short course ■ CPVA for families workshop ■

As shown in Chart 17, reflective of training offered to 115 parent/ carers, Non-Violent

Resistance is the most employed intervention provided. Parent/ carers indicated that this in

itself was not without problems, such as needing to self-fund or delays in accessing NVR

training for example:

- *I self funded an introductory NVR course on managing meltdowns with Sarah Fisher. I plan to do another in the spring. I've done this all off my own back. I did a parenting course with Coram (funded by ASF) but that didn't deal so much with violence and she was younger then and hadn't become so much of an issue*
- *NVR was given by family support worker*
- *We have done some ourselves through our therapist and practice nvr*
- *Applied for ASF funding for NVR training, still waiting for training to take place 6 months later*
- *Did NVR workshop recently and would have been helpful many years ago.*
- *NVR 10 week course was really useful for me and partner.  I funded a day course, then applied for funding from placing authority, which the CSW agreed. She left and I have been chased for the payment ever since!*
- *No - have asked frequently.  NVR not available in Scotland*
- *Was put on waiting list for NVR  12 months ago. Still waiting*

The overall consensus from parent/carers was that Non-Violent Resistance did help most of

these families but it was not a one size fits all, in that for some parent/ carers there was little

change and they were left disappointed having been led to understand this would resolve the

conflict within the home for them by professionals advising them:

- *Offered an introduction to NVR but no course in our area. Not sure it was right approach anyway for our children's needs.*
- *NVR via CAMHS but using an outdated model so not as good as we hoped*
- *NVR. Has to be used appropriately however and was not what decreased the behaviour*
- *Had NVR training through our post adoption social worker. Sadly it didn't work for us*
- *NVR training provided by ……. One day course but trainer was ill and we felt the day was unhelpful. It was funded by social services*
- *Tried NVR but problems escalated*

This leaves parent/carers in a difficult position, in that if intervention is offered, appropriate or

not, it can then be argued that it has been offered; this approach towards a health condition,

as conduct disorders are, does not resonate with approaches to physical health conditions. If a

treatment for a physical health condition is ineffective further solutions are sought, an approach that appears to be lacking in mental health (conduct disorder) conditions. This is supported by the number of those offered training who were placed onto 'positive parenting programmes' or similar, as shown in chart 17. In addition to those undertaking the Positive Parenting Programme, other 'parenting' programmes provided included:

- Therapeutic Parenting – 10 parent/ carers
- Parenting Back to Front – 1 parent/ carer
- PACE – 4 parent/ carers
- Theraplay- 3 parent/ carers
- Family therapy – 1 parent/carer
- Incredible Years Programme- 1 parent/ carer
- Parenting difficult teens- 1 parent/ carer

Such offers of training are not met with enthusiasm by parent/ carers overall for example:

- *We get offered generic parenting programmes all the time. They are rather patronising*
- *Triple P 8 years ago - totally inappropriate.*
- *My husband and I sought out and attended a parenting class but I did not find it helpful really. We were already doing a lot of the things advised. It made me feel alone.*
- *Triple P - but hasn't really helped*

The fundamental problem that arises within this for parent/ carers, appears to reflect what is available in the area rather than what the family need as a coping strategy. Such an approach is neither cost-effective or supportive if it does not meet the family's needs, and as noted within the comments, isolates families further which can then lead to families struggling unsupported in future having lost faith in professional capacity to help support them. Outside of self-funding, these courses are paid for through public funding be this Adoption Support Funding directly or via the local Authority; it is therefore a professional responsibility to be accountable for such expenditure, in so much as ensuring the right level of support and training is provided not solely that which is available locally, irrespective of the programme or courses ability to meet the needs of the family. Outside of 'parenting' programmes specifically targeted programme support that seeks to help families cope with the conduct disorder or cope with the violence were also noted by parent/ carers, although the number attending was negligible compared to the number of families requiring this support. Support offered to families targeting the behaviour more readily, rather than the parents 'parenting' capacity included:

- CPVA for family 'workshops'- 10 parent/ carers

- Therapeutic Crisis Intervention- 6 parent/ carers

- Multi-Systematic Theraplay- 2 parent/ carers

- Dyadic Developmental Psychotherapy (DDP)- 4 parent carers

- Great Behaviour Breakdown Training- 5 parent/ carers

- Attachment theory/ Awareness Training- 6 parent/ carers
- Anger Management- 1 parent/ carer
- Sensory Integration- 1 parent carer
- Secondary Trauma Processing- 1 parent carer
- PDA challenging Behaviour- 1 parent/ carer
- Riding the Rapids Course – 2 parent carers
- Cygnet Course- 4 parent/ carers
- Understanding challenging behaviour- 1 parent/ carer
- De-escalation techniques- 1 parent/ carer
- Team Teach- 1 parent/carer
- SafeBase- 1 parent/ carer

The purpose of identifying the range of training offered to one family out of the 538, who responded to the 2018 CPVA survey, highlights the sporadic and inconsistent approach used to date to support families living with CPVA. Such difference in what is offered supports argument of an ad hoc approach across those families living with CPVA. This suggests when seeking support one family in three may be offered training to help them manage their child's behaviour, but the quality and content may not match what they need, rather it is what is available locally. Such indicators also highlight the urgent need for formulating a real-world policy to inform professionals of pathways to supporting these families prior to crisis arising or the behaviour becoming entrenched or escalating. Moreover, such indicators reinforce the need to include these families specifically in any development of a training programme families can access that will meet the needs of the family; whilst also recognising a one size fits all approach is the most ineffective way forward as stated by parent/ carers:

- *We have been in receipt of a lot of DDP therapy and have changed our parenting considerably in line with this. However, whilst this approach works well for child 1, it is less effective for child 2.*

- *Awareness of CPV. Skimming surface no real suggestions other than platitudes.*

- *DDP is what is helping most so far when very narrow window of tolerance allows. Child's needs were not recognised until way too late and having to fight for understanding and support.*

- *No well Theroplay but that doesn't help with the violence*

- *team teach it wasn't very good. Nice but not for real situations. turning someone's elbow away when they are screaming in your face or throwing bedroom furniture at you isn't quite what you need*

- *Went in a child to parent violence workshop paid for by the ASF. It offered no practical strategies unfortunately, just talked about the reasons behind it. Got approval for NVR but was unable*

- *ASD Parent group at GOSH - very helpful. Parent group at residential school - very helpful. Did NVR workshop recently and would have been helpful many years ago.*

- *I've done 'anger management for high functioning autism' run by Gloucestershire carers. An NAS course*

- *secondary trauma processing with psychotherapist working with family before ASF FAL introduced, now no parent support; and weekly family therapy sessions for oldest. Youngests' play therapist had sessions with us until placing authority stopped funding.*

- *we have had to pay for our own training on PDA and challenging behaviour / anxiety. The autism team offered one 6 week parent course on ASD.*

Such comments recognise parents as being informed and aware of what they need and what works for their family, that does not reflect some of the suggestions made to families by professionals when seeking support, parent/ carers point to ill-informed suggestions made to them by professionals from predominantly Children's Services including:

- *Naughty step/ time out*

- *Offered training if I paid for it*

- *Only parenting courses but they said we knew everything so were more skilled in our parenting approach*

- *Assessed by Children's Learning Disability Service and given a behavioural plan to follow*

- *Told it was normal and that we had to put up with it*

- *Constantly ask but just given a pat on back and told we are doing a good job*

- *Training is not allowed because if something goes wrong it would be their fault*

- *Lent a book*

- *I also highlighted to medical team some trigger points when Ritalin wears off (adhd) and was told "well that's tough - aggression at night towards you is the pay off for better behaviour during the day at School". I fail to see why my health and well-being should be the "trade off" for my sons difficulties and why that hasn't elicited any support - until I got so upset I contacted social services myself.*

- *asked for this but was informed children's services knew nothing about it*

- *The training provided by our LA is outdated (eg reward charts) and is not in-depth enough to help effectively with CPV. I've been on NVR training - paid for by the ASF but instigated and arranged by myself - but there are no professionals within the LA who are trained in it and able to support with putting it into place within families. And the course wasn't very well taught.*

Whilst good practice within empirical research reporting can dismiss the findings as invalid and unreliable, due to the limited personal nature of these parent/ carer experiences, if only 1 parent out of the 538 responding is offered the training, then valid reliable data would be difficult to find, due to limited evaluation for such provision. To develop support and interventions gathering parent/ carer opinion appeared essential in order to move the CPVA 'issue' forward. Parent/carers are very clear in what they feel would help to support them in managing their child who displays CPVA and managing their own health and wellbeing, as well as that of others within the family home. The highest placed requirement, when calculated on word usage within responses is that of 'respite' care; which, if reflecting on the cost to the family economically and emotionally is understandable. However, respite care is difficult, in that there are far more children requiring respite care then there is availability, leaving families waiting for long periods to access this. One solution would be to look to Foster Carers already employed with the Authority or Private organisations, a practice some areas provide but not all. Seeking short term respite support from Foster Care may help build the basis for supporting these families, if such respite is for weekends or school holiday periods; this would enable those considering providing respite to retain their own employment outside of this brief 'break' period where need be. A further option is within the wider family, to enable this option to develop, support must be offered for the whole family, this in turn will strengthen relationships within the family, including wider family members. Whilst respite may be costly at a time when efficiencies are being made, this may provide the basis for keeping families together; in considering reducing services such as respite, Local Authorities need to consider if they are adequately resourced to provide for the child should the child be placed within their care via a S20, when the family is no longer able to keep the child at home. Alternatively, support could be provided within the home, be this with daily routines or within specific areas, a support intervention parents have highlighted rarely happens and is not available to them. In terms of professional requirement, parent/carers would ask that they are believed and not dismissed, so much so they feel this is the fundamental core area that must be explicit in any policy, guideline or pathway developed. Building on being believed and effectively listened to, parent/carers also request that all professionals are trained and knowledgeable, respond in a timely fashion, provide a contact point that covers 24 hours 7 days a week and support parent requests for training for families. These parent/ carers appreciate that services are not available 24 hours a day - 7 days a week and are often short staffed, what they request is that there is a team around them and their child, which may include the Police, Children's Services, Health Services, GPs and Teachers, similar to the Mobius Approach[43] of support, so that they are provided a named person they can contact should they need to, day or night. This would reduce the necessity to seek police intervention as crisis response if, or when, the behaviour escalates and would provide support from an informed Multi-Agency team, thereby reflecting the 'wrap around' approach needed.

Building on these suggestions parent/carers suggested nine main areas they would include about CPVA in any good practice pathways, policies or guidelines for helping professionals to support families living with CPVA. The first of these is for professionals to understand and appreciate what CPVA actually is, and that this is not just 'normative behaviour'. This suggestion reflects that detailed within Sections 4 and 5 of this report, particularly for those parents living not only with CPVA but a child who has been diagnosed with a conduct disorder. Alongside this the second suggestion is to engage in active listening rather than 'listening but not hearing' when parent/ carers raise CPVA as an issue within the home. Such active listening is the fundamental basis for developing an understanding of what CPVA is for families and would be the basis of any referral towards the child being assessed, for the World Health Organisation F.91-0 categories of conduct disorder, directly related to behaviours within the family. Parent/carers are very clear in their third recommendation, they state there is a real and urgent need for professionals, supporting families living with CPVA, to undertake training in CPVA, so that they are able to provide an empathetic approach. Without such training professionals rely on their own understanding and see CPVA through their own 'professional'

---

[43] See Brandt K (2014) Rethinking Therapeutic Work: Transdisciplinary Therapy in Infant-Family & Early Childhood Mental Health. Child Trauma Academy

lens which may or may not be well-informed but is open to bias and presumption based on a sympathetic approach rather than an empathetic approach at best.

The fourth suggestion parent/carers ask is that guidance is developed for all professionals and support workers involved in the family unit overall detailing clear pathways. Moving the current definition of CPVA outside of all children who engage in CPVA behaviours enables recognition of the two distinct but different definitions of CPVA and is the foundation towards developing these guidelines. For those children who display CPVA as intentional behaviour the Home Office and the Criminal Justice Act (1998) provide pathways for professionals to adhere to; however, it is not unreasonable to suggest these children are the minority of children who engage in CPVA, as opposed to the majority of children who display CPVA without intention, as a consequence of a diagnosable Conduct Disorder that is displayed in the family.  It is these families who require clear guidance for professionals to be written, to enable professionals to understand the distinct difference between those children who engage in CPVA intentionally and those who do not. This 'guidance' would then meet the parent/carers fifth request, that professionals work effectively with families and understand this has to be felt to be effective by the families they engage with. In doing so professionals are then able to reflect the sixth area parent/ carers pointed to that resonates with decision making based on information rather than presumption. Parent/ carers agree that professionals should find out about any underlying condition rather than presume to know what CPVA means to families and presume to determine that all children displaying CPVA do so intentionally, which is not the case for the majority of children displaying CPVA. In this way it is recommended that when any CPVA is reported to professionals, irrespective of where they practice, they determine if the child has a diagnosable conduct disorder or is being assessed for a conduct disorder. Professionals then equip themselves with the details outlined within Section 4 of this report, to enable them to determine frequency and behaviour displayed. These records should detail the *Antecedent*, the *Behaviour* and the *Consequences* of the behaviour; for example, did anyone require medical attention, are items within the home broken, what damage if any was there to persons within the home including siblings, what damage is there to the home or contents. Parent/ carers need reassurance that such records are not being collected in order to formalise a criminal prosecution, or to determine their ability as a parent, rather that these records are part of the process in determining any Conduct Disorder the child may have.

The seventh suggestion from parent/ carers is that professionals update what training is available, how effective the training is according to parent/ carers undertaking the training and offer relevant training to parents in a timely fashion to reduce the risk of the behaviour becoming entrenched or escalating. Moreover, such training should not be seen as a 'fix' for CPVA, and in line with 'treatments' for physical medical conditions if the intervention is not effective, to re-evaluate completely and seek and alternative training for the family without prejudice. The eighth area parent/ carers feel is a main aspect of professional support is that professionals to know how and where to access funding, to enable interventions and training to be financed for families. For those families who live with children who engage in CPVA unintentionally, the diagnosis of a conduct disorder will enable funding to be allocated via the NHS, however funding for children with mental health indicators is a real concern across the UK at this time, therefore, professionals may need to consider alternative avenues and this information should be available to parent/carers without the need for the parent/carer to search and source funding, or bring this to the attention of professionals; examples of funding should include the Adoption Support Fund, funding offered by Charitable organisations and uses for Pupil Premium where this is provided to schools. Developing these main areas requested by parent/ carers will enable professionals to meet the ninth area parent/ carers have noted. Parent/ Carers have stated they need professionals to act rather than talk about CPVA, they require professionals not only to advise them of options but do follow through discussions and ensure decisions are acted upon.

With reference to what parent/ carers, responding to this 2018 CPVA survey feel is the main thing they would include about CPVA, in a guide for other parents is summarised into three main points. These parent/carers would advise other parents and families to:

- Shout out- speak up – be heard
- Join support groups
- Do training

In shouting out- speaking up and being heard, these parent/ carers reduce the impact of what Holt (ibid) noted. Holt *(ibid)* pointed to paradigm shift in what childhood means in contemporary society today arguing that when discussing CPVA there is

*A factor that perhaps is unique to this kind of abuse is the 'culture of blame', which has intensified over the past decade in relation to parenting. There is much evidence that this cultural climate has shaped both parental and societal responses to the problematic behaviour of children and young people.* (p. 187)

Moreover, these three recommendations, proposed by parent/ carers enable parents to reflect what Jakob (2018) highlighted, that an increasing parental presence is a vital component in helping families to manage and cope and requires a social support network.

**Section Summary**

This section presents what parent/ carers living with CPVA feel works and what does not. This section reflects on training offered to date to those responding within the 2018 CPVA survey and points to a fragmented ad hoc approach to supporting families, that is nether helpful or effective. Training offered to families is dependent on where they live and what is available in the area, rather than what is needed. Furthermore, many parent/ carers wait unreasonable lengthy times to receive this training due to funding indicators. The impact of developing discussion about the reality of CPVA for families is viewed with a mixed response by parent/ carers. For many parent/ carers opening up discussion has been helpful and reduced feelings of guilt about being 'to blame' for their child's behaviour, enabling them to feel less alone and supporting them when seeking help. Alternatively, for others, media coverage has sensationalised CPVA in unhelpful ways and has led to advice being provided by one and all, irrespective of their experience, knowledge or understanding of what CPVA is. This section outlines the suggestions parent/ carers indicate would promote good practice by professionals and help other parent/ carers who find themselves living with CPVA.  In this way this section outlines 'where next' and points to action rather than more discussion. In summary this section points to nine suggestions that parent/carers highlight is needed in order to support them and their family collectively:

1. Professionals to understand and appreciate what CPVA actually is.
2. Professionals to engage in active listening rather than 'listening but not hearing' when parent/ carers raise CPVA as an issue within the home.
3. Professionals supporting families living with CPVA to undertake training in CPVA;
4. CPVA guidance is developed for all professionals and support workers involved in the family unit overall to follow and recognise, detailing clear pathways.

5. Professional to work effectively with families and understand this has to be felt to be effective by the families they engage with.
6. Professional decision making based on information and knowledge rather than presumption.
7. Professionals undertake CPVA training and offer relevant training to parents in a timely fashion.
8. Professionals to know how and where to access funding to enable interventions and training to be financed for families.
9. Professionals to act rather than talk about CPVA, they require professionals not only to advise them of options but do follow through discussions and ensure decisions are acted upon.

# Section 8 - Lets Talk About

## Reflections on Child to Parent Violence and Aggression

In 2017 when Thorley and Coates published their survey for participant responses the following definition was employed to define CPVA: *'Any harmful act by a child, whether physical, psychological or financial, which is intended to gain power and control over a parent or carer'* (Cottrell, 2001) and in this way, accepted and recognised this definition as the one used most frequently within publications and discussions around Child on Parent Violence or Aggression, irrespective of how CPVA was 'labelled'. Within responses received by Thorley and Coates (2017a, b, c) the issue of defining Child on Parent Violence and Aggression (CPVA) became more difficult to establish, as outlined within their reports. It became increasingly evident that many responders felt the term was not applicable to their children due to how they, the respondent, understood the term 'intent'. This reflected the basic nuance and juxtaposition that exposes the difficulties of using anonymous surveys within research as a method of data collection. With the benefit of hindsight, the use of that definition raised personal issues for some respondents, that then precluded their participation, in that these individuals felt the definition did not apply to them or their child. Such difficulties reflect the basis of hermeneutics, in that word usage, application and meaning can be associated with dialectical appreciation between text/ reader and reader/ response (Osborne 1991). Robinson (1995) acknowledges the conflict arising between the conducting of research and the reporting of research when attempting to project data into text (what data the research is attempting to generate through survey questions and how these are decoded and understood by those responding highlights how this conflict may occur)[44]. In this sense, hermeneutics helps to explain why survey questions can be difficult for some respondents, particularly when using wording such as 'intent' and 'intended', whereby those responding may feel their child's actions were not deliberately 'intended' in a planned approach, rather they were unintended and unplanned (as argued in Thorley and Coates, 2017c). Prospective contributors explained that there was a level of discomfort with the definition and this was primarily focused on the use of the words 'intent' and 'control'. Parents and carers felt that the definition applied within the Thorley and Coates (2017) survey did not reflect their individual family or circumstance; and though they acknowledged that they were experiencing violence and aggression, this definition became a stumbling block for them when the completed the survey. Moreover, concern's over application of the definition, reflecting Cottrell's position, was also raised by a notable number of attendees at CPVA events, that were held to share the findings of the survey through verbal interaction and focus group discussions, following publication of the survey reports (Thorley and Coates 2017c). Parents and carers who attended the presentations acknowledged that violence and aggression was a significant issue but felt very strongly the definition employed within the survey (*ibid.*) did not reflect their experience, in relation to the motivation of the child who engaged in this type of behaviour. They argued that it was their own personal belief that their child was not behaving intentionally and had no 'intent to control'. The anecdotal experience from decoding the survey (*ibid*) corroborated the view of those focus group attendees and highlighted that parents do not perceive their experience as being that of other parents because of the definition offered (Eckstein,2016). This was further evidenced within correspondence received, following the publications of the reports (*ibid*), that emphasised the behaviour resonated with many families but the definition offered did not. With such a high level of anecdotal concern, regarding the definition, the CPVA survey 2018 was designed to include the opportunity for participants to offer their own definition, based upon their own experiences, that provided insight into what CPVA meant to them and their family.

---

[44] Such dilemma's reflect Gadamer's suggestions around philosophical hermeneutics whereby human understanding remains irrevocably biased due to the personalised nature of individual human understanding

Cottrell's 2001 definition comes from her work on the specific issue of abuse of parents by teenage children and of itself is an accurate description of the phenomena; as highlighted in a significant number of academic works that followed[45]. The definition suggested by Cottrell (2001) has been employed and embedded into targeted behaviour management programmes for CPVA, such as Non-Violent Resistance (NVR) (Coogan & Lauster, 2015). However, the continued use of this definition then focuses responses towards CPVA management that can rely on conscious behaviour change, rather than sub-conscious behaviour response; in addition, this also focuses CPVA research towards the behaviour of older children and adolescents (Coogan, 2011), that fails to recognise similar behaviour in younger children under adolescence age. Though this work addressing CPVA and supporting families living with CPVA is valued and significant, the findings of Thorley and Coates (2017 a, b and c) identified incidents of CPVA in children predominantly younger than adolescents; with the majority age range reflecting those children aged 6-11 years, rather than those children over 12 years of age. Moreover, their indicators suggested that the issue of CPVA was just as notable in children under aged 5 years, as it was for those over aged 12 years. The issue of CPVA for children rather than adolescents was one of the key findings noted within their reports (*ibid*). When reflecting on the issue of CPVA displayed by children, against the discomfort that many contributors had indicated about the definition, it suggested that more data and information should be generated if understanding is to be developed. Such exploration needed to encompass CPVA behaviours displayed by those children under the age of adolescence, that appeared to be the majority of families living with CPVA. Exploring parent and carer's insights, as well as their individual position, regarding their own child's motivations or triggers for the behaviour displayed, were essential to providing appreciation of the phenomena and definition of CPVA. Maclean and Harrison (2009) describe individuals as 'experts of their own experience' and certainly within this context the views of parents and carers, on why their children are violent or aggressive, has value. In offering a definition that accurately encompasses a wider range of parent and carer's experience can provide the basis to develop understanding and good practice responses, in this way such understanding can quantifying the phenomena and highlight when intervention should occur as a proactive approach.

---

[45] see for example, Walsh and Krienert, 2007; Sung Hong *et al*, 2012; Calvete *et al*, 2013; Patuleia *et al*, 2013; , Ibabe *et al*, 2013; Fréchette *et al*, 2015; Lyons' Bell *et al*, 2015; Contreras and del Carmen Cano, 2016; Ibabe and Bentler, 2016; Gerard, 2017; Kuay *et al*, 2017)

Selwyn and Meakins (2015) noted that the lack of a standardised definition is one barrier to accurately quantifying the scale and level of violence perpetrated by children against adult parents or carers. This was seen as an opportunity to develop an insight into adult's perceptions, of the motivations and triggers relating to the violence and aggression that they individually experienced, in order to explore the definition as being fit for purpose, that applied to all families living with CPVA. Such exploration would then enable all families to feel the outline of what CPVA is resonates with them and their experience. Including all families living with CPVA is an essential component of ascertaining the extent of CPVA for families within society, as well as the basis for forming good practice responses and any potential early intervention approaches. This was developed through 2 specific questions pertaining the definition currently used. The first question asked if they felt Cottrell's 2001 definition ''*Any harmful act by a child, whether physical, psychological or financial, which is intended to gain power and control over a parent or carer'* accurately described child to parent violence in their own opinion. In the most basic terms, from the 538 responses received, the data indicated that 31.7% (171 participants) felt that the definition accurately describes the CPVA they themselves experienced, however the majority indicated that it was either incorrect or only partly accurate as highlighted within the chart 18

Chart 18
Do you feel the description of what CPVA/ APVA is accurately describes
child on parent violence or aggression

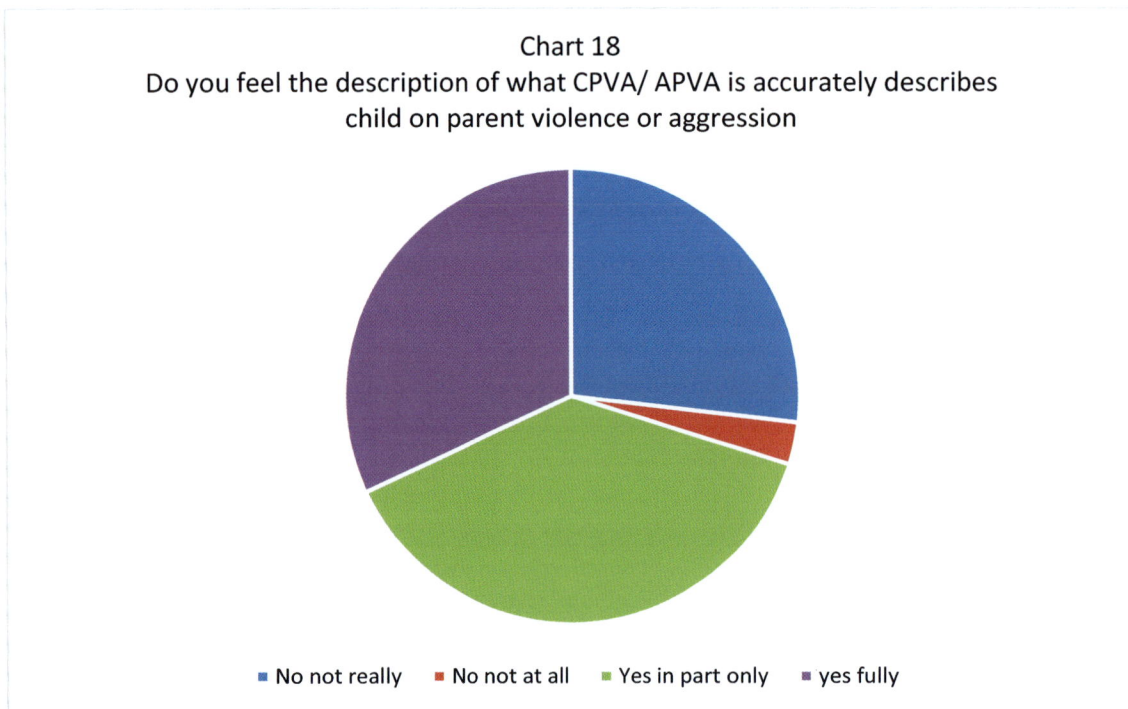

■ No not really    ■ No not at all    ■ Yes in part only    ■ yes fully

Within the 2018 CPVA survey, all respondents indicating 'no not really', 'no not at all', or 'yes in part only', were then pointed to an open answer question that asked: 'If you do not feel the definition is accurate what would you change this to be?' This generated 320 responses to be generated, all of which allowed for the individual parental voice to be recorded. Though the individual answers were unique and personalised, several themes were repeated, these were the use of 'intent' and the use of 'control'. Within the thematic areas identified one area was overwhelmingly represented and contested, this was the inclusion, within the definition, that the purpose of the behaviour was *to gain power and control over the parent*. Participants were clear in their disagreement of this terminology, as shown in the following for example:

- *'My child is violent as a response to her anxiety or sensory issues. There is no intent to control or to exert power'*
- *'In our case it is a meltdown from frustration or anxiety and is not to gain power or control.'*
- *'I don't believe my child has any control over his violence & it certainly isn't to gain power'*

These respondents acknowledged violent, aggressive and challenging behaviour but felt clearly that there was no intent to gain power and control over the caregiver. This was a significant theme that was developed by the majority of respondents. A number of the responses offered no insight or alternative to the given definition but suggested that the words 'intent' and 'control' be removed; several parent/carers noted that the inclusion of *'control'* and *'intent'* reflected abusive relationships that they felt uncomfortable with, as they believed this did not accurately reflect their child or their child's behaviour. Similar indicators of not seeing oneself as a victim has been noted previously for parent/carers living with CPVA, for example Eckstein (2016) asserted parents can be reluctant to identify or acknowledge incidents as 'abuse', consequently parent/carers do not then see themselves as 'abused'. That parents and carers are reluctant to label their children as abusive should be of little surprise; however, their reluctance dilutes the impact of their lived experience and circumstances. When grouping the individual responses, the second largest group felt that the intent to control was part of the motivation or trigger and agreed with the definition in part.

- *'this is not about gaining control over a parent but control over a situation that they feel they are not in control of'*
- *'lashing out as a way of controlling their environment; either to prevent further stress or to reduce sensory overload.'*
- *'she wants to gain control over her situation as a way to counter her overwhelming anxiety and difficulty dealing with the world'*

This reframes the violence as less of a personal attack purposefully directed at a parent or caregiver to control them; rather the attack as incidental or part of the child's employed strategy to control their environment. In this way what parent/carers recognise is that whilst their child may engage in CPVA, the current understanding of what CPVA is does not reflect their child. Such suggestions by parent/ carers of their child's behaviour and reasons for this point to the indicators for the World Health Organisations international categories with particular reference to Conduct Disorders within the family, outlined within ICD-10 (ICD-11) as F91.0. Reframing parental responses and mapping these within ICD-10/11 indicators provides parents with a manifestation of their child's behaviour; as opposed to 'fitting' the child into a generally held understanding that does not reflect their child.  This nuance is further highlighted within the parent/ carer responses, where parent/ carers clearly point to co-morbidity of known conduct disorder difficulties their child has, for example: *'I think the use of 'intended' is difficult because very often violence and aggression can be unintentional but brought about by external and internal triggers that my child has no control over'.* This response sums up the two factors that parent/ carers feel is an essential element of understanding and defining the violence and aggression that they personally experience. The views of parent/ carers detailed within the 2018 CPVA survey, of their child and their child's behaviour, resonates with previous reports and publications; for example: Baker *et* al (2003), Anderson (2011), Calvete *et* al (2012), Collins (2015), Boorman (2016), Brule and Eckstein (2016), Adoption UK (2017), Breman and MacRea (2017), Coates (2017). What is evident in the narrative of parents, and the research and reports noted, is the existence of a Conduct Disorder that these children have. Such indicators are repeated in this 2018 CPVA survey in that all of the following were noted within Chart 10:

- Attachment difficulties including Reactive Attachment Disorder,
- Learning Difficulties (mild, moderate and profound) including Communication Difficulties (speech and language)
- Global Developmental Delay
- Foetal Alcohol spectrum Disorder (FASD)
- Autistic Spectrum Disorder (ASD)
- Mental Health Indicators including Anxiety, Depression, Post-Traumatic Stress disorder, special Educational Mental Health (SEMH) Emotional and Behavioural Difficulties (EBD)
- Experience of Trauma including Post Traumatic Stress Disorder and Complex Trauma
- Attention Deficit Hyperactivity Disorder

Moreover, parent/ carers reported co-morbid conduct disorders that informed their child's behaviour, for this reason, it appears evident that any displays of CPVA behaviours need to be seen as part of the childs health needs, rather than a trait of a known condition. Recognising that CPVA can be viewed as a Conduct Disorder diagnosable within ICD-10/11 conditions provides the basis of separating CPVA into that displayed which is intentional and seeks to 'control' and that which is unintentional and does not seek to 'control'.  It is this, the second definition, provided for by the World Health Organisation:

> ***Conduct disorder confined to the family context:*** *Conduct disorder involving dissocial or aggressive behaviour (and not merely oppositional, defiant, disruptive behaviour), in which the abnormal behaviour is entirely, or almost entirely, confined to the home and to interactions with members of the nuclear family or immediate household. The disorder requires that the overall criteria for F91.- be met; even severely disturbed parent-child relationships are not of themselves sufficient for diagnosis.*

that recognises the behaviour displayed and reported by these families, where the CPVA displayed is without intention.  Moreover, the criteria for meeting the World Health Organisation listing F91, as a pre-requisite for *'Conduct disorder confined to the family context'* to be diagnosed, reflects the behaviour parent/ carers detail:

> ***Conduct Disorders: (F.91)*** *Disorders characterized by a repetitive and persistent pattern of dissocial, aggressive, or defiant conduct. Such behaviour should amount to major violations of age-appropriate social expectations; it should therefore be more severe than ordinary childish mischief or adolescent rebelliousness and should imply an enduring pattern of behaviour (six months or longer). Features of conduct disorder can also be symptomatic of other psychiatric conditions, in which case the underlying diagnosis should be preferred.*
> *Examples of the behaviours on which the diagnosis is based include excessive levels of fighting or bullying, cruelty to other people or animals, severe destructiveness to property, fire-setting, stealing, repeated lying, truancy from school and running away from home, unusually frequent and severe temper tantrums, and disobedience. Any one of these behaviours, if marked, is sufficient for the diagnosis, but isolated dissocial acts are not.*

The importance of listening to parent/ carers is evident within the responses received for the 2018 CPVA survey, in that parent/ carers discuss that their children have a number of underlying potential 'triggers' for engaging in CPVA including anxiety, fear, panic, frustration dysregulation, disassociation, being overwhelmed, stress, inability to express emotions, sensory distress, loss of control, impact of trauma and inability to process emotions. These indicators and triggers sit within the range of cognitive and neurological disorders outlined, as well as a range of emotional and psychological impairments detailed within responses. It is therefore unsurprising that this cohort of children living with the parent/carers participating in the 2018 CPVA survey (irrespective of if they were birth parents, adoptive parents, kinship carers, foster carers or guardians) struggle to behave or moderate their behaviour as desired by 'normative' indicators, as detailed by parent/carer responses:

- *'my child shows aggression towards me it absolutely isn't to gain control but it is because his emotions are so extremely out of control that this is the only way he can express himself.'*

- *'Not being able to self-regulate and turn to lashing out as a way of controlling their environment; either to prevent further stress or to reduce sensory overload.'*

- *'I feel sometimes my child's anger can be frustration in not being understood. (He has a severe speech delay)'*

These insights into why children engage in CPVA help inform the policy and practice that needs to be built in order to support these families effectively. Whilst it is recognised the Home Office Guidance (2015) is for Adolescents who intend to use CPVA behaviour, in order to gain control, there is little alternative guidance available at this time for the majority of children displaying CPVA. This means these parents, living with CPVA, have no real support pathway, as CPVA displayed within the home, prior to adolescent is not the responsibility of any one service provision if we continue to see these children as behaving intentionally and in ways needed to seek control. It is therefore necessary to re-evaluate the gaps in service provision. Whilst the Police are recognised as supportive and helpful, it is in reality the Health Service who need to provide the support these families require, through Mental Health Services. There may continue to be a need for families to contact the Police should the safety of other children in the home be of concern, or the level of violence is such they require immediate response. Once involved, the Police can enquire about existing Conduct Disorders and help refer the family to the relevant support service. This will also reduce the number of children, with Conduct Disorders, being placed in the custody of the Police, where this is clearly not the appropriate place for children with Conduct Disorders who are struggling with internalised impacts leading to their externalised behaviour.

The second element of the 'intent and control' theme related to the range of external stimulations that 'triggered' the children's violent, challenging and aggressive behaviour. External indicators include: social situations, transitions, change, noise, sensation, school, boundaries, demands and expectations that these children's peers may not find difficulty in managing if their peers did not have a Conduct Disorder or Learning need. The external influences impacting on internalised and externalised behaviours were identified by several respondents as individually or collectively, that precipitated dysregulation and deterioration in the child's behaviour, which in turn left the child resorting to the strategy of challenging, violent and aggressive behaviour as CPVA. In this way it is not unexpected for the child to engage in CPVA if they have high stress responses within their neurological development, a known outcome of Adverse Childhood Experiences, as outlined by Perry (1995, 1998, 2006, 2013, 2016) and within the Polyvagal theory (2001, 2003) alongside Adverse Childhood Experience findings. High stress response (Toxic Stress[46]) places the child in a sub-conscious survival position, following which the child will display 'fight' or 'flight 'or 'freeze'; therefore it is not a conscious intentional behaviour the child displays, at this moment in time when engaging is CPVA, as previously highlighted by Thorley and Coates (2017c). Such 'reactive' behaviour resonate of 'survival behaviour' is not resonate with CPVA as it is currently understood, highlighting the need to reframe understanding of what CPVA is and distinguish between those behaviours that are displayed with intent and those that are not. This is further evidenced within discussion about new understanding for children's behaviours and the relationship between Adverse Childhood Experiences and behaviour, outlined by the National Scientific Council on the Developing Child (2005/ 2014, p.5)

> *Science does not support the claim that infants and young children are too young to be affected by significant stresses that negatively affect their family and caregiving environments. To the contrary, human studies with infants and children as well as animal studies have shown that adverse early infant experiences (e.g., neglectful maternal care) and serious disruptions of the prenatal environment (e.g., drug and alcohol exposure)* **can lead to short-term neurobehavioral and neurohormonal changes in offspring that may have long-term adverse effects on memory, learning, and behavior** *throughout life.* (my emphaisis)

It can therefore, be anticipated, that those children who have a high Adverse Childhood Experience score are more at risk of engaging in CPVA both in the early years and throughout their childhood, as opposed to their counterparts who have a lower ACE score, including those children who are Looked After or have been Previously Looked After and now reside with Adoptive parents, Kinship carers or Special Guardians. This helps to explain why Adoptive

---

[46] 'toxic Stress' is a term developed by Shankoff at the Centre on the Developing Child (Harvard University) to differentiate between levels of stress that occur in the norm and those that result in high stress response activation from early Adverse Childhood Experiences, see for example: Shonkoff, J. P., & Garner, A. (2012). The lifelong effects of early childhood adversity and toxic stress. *Pediatrics, 129*(1), e232–e246.

parent/ carers statistically report CPVA more frequently than other parent groups, in that by default the children they are parenting will have a higher ACE score leading to the decision of Adoption as the best outcome for the child.

In addition to the potential higher levels of prevalence, for those children with high Adverse Childhood Experience indicators, where children have been diagnosed with a Conduct Disorder that reflects difficulty controlling behaviour, or have been identified with difficulty in communicating, it would seem prudent to monitor behaviour for indicators of what is currently described as CPVA. This would then enable professionals and families to keep a 'diary' of events and commence from the basis of 'is this a co-morbid condition' rather than determine all behaviour to be 'part of' an existing condition. It would also promote early identification of co-morbidity that allows for specific interventions to be identified, rather than the current position of reflecting all CPVA under the same 'intentional' umbrella; which can lead to all CPVA behaviour, with or without intent, being perceived as a 'criminal' behaviour to be processed through 'Policing' the problem. The possibility of recognising CPVA as a conduct disorder, under World Health Indicators, has been available for some time and continues to be available to professionals supporting families living with CPVA, as a *'Conduct disorder confined to the family context'*. The real issue this raises is finding solutions to separating CPVA behaviours that are with intention, from those that are not. Collectively, less than a third of parents agreed the current definition, this suggests that how CPVA is perceived at present, to include intention and a desire to control, overlooks the reality for the majority of families within the 2018 CPVA study and their experience of living with CPVA. It is not unreasonable to propose that this finding is not unique to this 2018 CPVA study and was previously outlined by Adoption UK (2018) and well as Thorley and Coates (2017). Whilst those in agreement of the definition represented less than a third of parent/carers participating, it is important their views are also herd. Although in the minority, the level of abuse within the household is not an area that can be overlooked or dismissed as infrequent. These parent/carers, who agreed the definition reflected their experiences, also argued that the definition did little to recognise the level of abuse they were subjected too and this is the area they themselves would like developed into more detail. Developing a detailed definition that reflects these parent/ carer voices can be achieved, by accepting the behaviour outlined, displayed by children in this study.

**Section Summary**

The 2018 CPVA survey looked to view the respondents as experts by experience, recognising as such that they have offered a valuable insight to their lived experience. An underlying question that has to be considered when considering parent/ carers responses relates to the personalised level of their knowledge, experience and analysis of the causes of their child's challenging, violent and aggressive behaviour. Scourfield (2009) notes that experts by experience are only 'experts' of their area and of their specific lived experience; in this way it is recognised that such experiences are personalised to individuals and may not resonate with others. This can be addressed through more detailed qualitative studies, by interviewing the individual respondents and investigating their experiences. However, given the nature of the questions posed such depth of detail on a larger scale may be difficult to ascertain. For this reason, at this time and within this study, the perceptions and knowledge of the adult describing the incident have to be relied on as their truthfulness. This 'truthfulness' raises further difficulties, in that the parent/ carer may not want to acknowledge or perceive that they themselves maybe inadvertently contributing to triggering the incident, or that they themselves may not wish to acknowledge the behaviour as problematic.

Across all participant parent/carers there is broad agreement on what constitutes violence and aggression, however questions around motivation and underlying issues, that lead to violence and aggression, remained.  One aim of this study was to consider if the widely used definition *'Any harmful act by a child, whether physical, psychological or financial, which is intended to gain power and control over a parent or carer'* (Cottrell 2004) was considered appropriate, for the cohort of respondents within the adoption, fostering, special guardian and SEND community. In asking what a preferred definition would be, the purpose was not to prove Cottrell's definition as misleading or incorrect; rather, it was to develop discussions that have increasingly pointed to the definition as problematic in reflecting all CPVA behaviour displayed, for all children engaging in CPVA. What has transpired, within this 2018 CPVA survey, is that the global definition currently used does reflect CPVA behaviour for those children who intend to behave in this way, in order to have control over their parent/ carer. Furthermore, the global definition also provided this study the opportunity to discern between those children who engaged in CPVA with intention, to those children who displayed CPVA without intention, as proportionate of all of the children this study represents. The findings of this calculation clearly point to the majority of children display CPVA without intent. More importantly, underlying recognised indicators were highlighted for those children displaying

CPVA without intent; that enabled the behaviour to be considered within World Health Organisation F.91.0 *Conduct disorder confined to the family context* as a co-morbidity. This means that the current practice of identifying children who engage in CPVA as a collective group of children, irrespective of the child's individual history or health indicators, fails to meet the needs of the child and by association the needs of the family. Those children who engage in CPVA with intent are the minority group of children overall who display CPVA. This essential nuance of wording- intend to engage in CPVA or display CPVA- has provided the opportunity to interrogate causes for CPVA occurrence. In doing so this 2018 CPVA survey has evidenced that there are two distinct forms of CPVA, the first of which is demonstrative of the current understanding, reflecting the behaviour of some children. The second definition, reflective of the majority of children who 'display' CPVA, is that this unintentional reactive CPVA is situated within Conduct Disorders, as outlined by the World Health Organisation; and is founded in higher levels of Adverse Childhood Experiences or as a co-morbidity to an existing known behaviour or communication difficulty.  These findings do not render Cottrell's definition redundant, rather it confirms the definition as reflective of some children who engage in CPVA, and in this way represents one manifestation of the phenomena of children who are violent and aggressive to their parents or carers. With the developing knowledge of underlying triggers and causes of child violence, aggression and challenging behaviour; it is appropriate to designate differences in the underlying causes and circumstances that define it. Childhood Challenging, Violent and Aggressive Behaviour (CCVAB) describes children who are unable to regulate and moderate their verbal, emotional and physical responses to their environment or circumstances; subsequently the behaviour of these children becomes challenging, aggressive or violent. Removing the emotive language of 'parent' and 'child' enables the definition to apply to the wide range of home and family environments that children live within. It is proposed that this, or a similar definition, such as the application of the correct categorisation: ***Conduct disorder confined to the family context*** is incorporated into the public and professional discourse. As Holt's (2016) explains our definition of Child to Parent Violence shapes how we understand it and subsequently respond to it. Separating the two distinctive ways in which children demonstrate CPVA enables effective support to be provided. There is growing concern about the increasing numbers of children employing CPVA as a behaviour; whilst it may be that children are increasingly doing so, new emerging technologies, that encourage data and information sharing, may also be instrumental in these increasing numbers; for example, within social media, such as Twitter and Facebook, parents living with CPVA are able to connect with other parents, in ways that were previously unavailable. This in itself will encourage more open discussion of CPVA, CPVA causes and CPVA behaviours that in turn continue to provide insight into the lives of families living with CPVA. It is therefore unknown if CPVA is increasing, or if awareness of CPVA is increasing, or if the increase is a combination of both possibilities.

# References

- **ACE Study:** American health maintenance organization Kaiser Permanente and the Centers for Disease Control and Prevention (1995-1997) The Adverse Childhood Experiences Study (**ACE Study**) is a research **study** leading to a wide range of publications which are listed at: http://www.theannainstitute.org/ACE%20STUDY%20FINDINGS.html.
  NOTE: This study has been replicated internationally and is widely recognised for predicting future indicators for children as they progress to adulthood, for example see the The Public Health Wales NHS Report (2015) at: http://www.cph.org.uk/wp-content/uploads/2016/01/ACE-Report-FINAL-E.pdf ; and Liverpool Johns Moore University (2016) in their study from Hertfordshire, Luton and Northhamptonshire available at: http://www.cph.org.uk/wp-content/uploads/2016/05/Adverse-Childhood-Experiences-in-Hertfordshire-Lutonand-Northamptonshire-FINAL_compressed.pdf

- Achenbach, T. M., & Edelbrock, C. (1978). The classification of child psychopathology: A review and analysis of empirical efforts. *Psychological Bulletin*, 85, 1275-1301

- Adfam and Against Violence and Abuse (2012) Between a rock and a hard place: How parents deal with children who use substances and perpetrate abuse. Adfam and Against Violence and Abuse a project funded by the Department of Health, available at: http://www.adfam.org.uk/docs/Between_a_rock_and_a_hard_place__Project_report.pdf

- Adopter A, March 14 2017: Why broccoli isn't my biggest challenge as an adoptive parent: my CPV post: available at: https://lifewithboyandgirl.wordpress.com/2017/03/14/why-broccoli-isnt-my-biggest-challenge-as-an-adoptive-parent-my-cpvpost/

- Adoption UK  (2017) Trauma-fuelled violence *Advice from adopters and experts on how to deal with the challenge of aggressive behaviours.* Adoption UK. Adoption Today Magazine

- Alvesson M and Skoldberg K (2000) Reflexive Methodology London, Sage Publications

- Alvesson M and Skoldberg K (2001) Reflexive Methodology (reprinted) London, Sage Publications

- American Psychiatric Association (2013) The Diagnostic and Statistical Manual of Mental Disorders, Fifth Edition. published by the American Psychiatric Association

- Anderson C (2011) New Research on Children with ASD and Aggression Kennedy Krieger Institute (last updated November 2012)

- Baker BL, McIntyre LL, Blacher J, Crnic K, Edelbrock C, Low C. (2003) Pre-school children with and without developmental delay: behaviour problems and parenting stress over time. Journal of Intellectual Disability Research 2003 May-Jun;47(Pt 4-5):217-30

- Baumrind, D. (1966). Effects of Authoritative Parental Control on Child Behavior, Child Development, 37(4), 887-907.

- Berger P L and Luckmann T (1966) The Social Construction of Reality Garden City New York, Doubleday

- Blakemore S J (2012) the Mysterious Workings of the Teenage Brain https://www.ted.com/talks/sarah_jayne_blakemore_the_mysterious_workings_of_the_adolescent_brain

- Bonnick H (2016) Episode 3 - An interview with Helen Bonnick about CPV. Available at: http://adoptionandfostering.podbean.com/ 7th November 2016

- Boorman, A. (2016) Support For Violent Children: What Next? (Part One) https://allaboardthetraumatrain.com/2016/12/04/support-for-violent-children-what-next/

- Brandt K (2014) Rethinking Therapeutic Work: Transdisciplinary Therapy in Infant-Family & Early Childhood Mental Health. Child Trauma Academy

- Breman R and MacRae A (2017) *'It's been an absolute nightmare' Family violence in kinship care.* Baptcare 2017. August 2017.

- Broadhead S and Francis R, (2015) The Making of Good Men and Women: SUMMARY REPORT: Responding to Youth Violence in the Home and its harmful impacts on families and communities in Western Australia. Womens Health and Family Services. Available at: http://www.whfs.org.au/files/userfiles/11898%20%20The%20making%20of%20good%20men%20and%20women%20reportONLINE.PDF

- Bronfenbrenner, U. (1979). The ecology of human development: Experiments by nature and design. Cambridge, MA: Harvard University Press.

- Brule N J and Eckstein J J (2016) "Am I Really A Bad Parent?": Adolescent to Parent Abuse (AtPA) Identity and the Stigma Management Communication (SMC) Model. Journal of Family Communication

- Bryman A (2015) Social Research Methods. Oxford University Press

- Bulmer M (1977) Sociological Research Methods. Transaction publishers

- Calvete E, Orue I and Gámez-Guadix M (2012) Child-to-Parent Violence: Emotional and Behavioral Predictors. Journal of Interpersonal Violence. 28(4) 755–772

- Caspi J (2011) Sibling Aggression: Assessment and Treatment. Springer Publishing

- Cassidy S (2012) Rise in parents terrorised by their children. The Independent. 17th February 2012

- Childrens Commissioner (2017) Childrens voices: A review of evidence on the subjective wellbeing of children involved in gangs in England. The childrens Commissioner, November 2017

- Coates, A. (2017) My experience of living with child-on-parent violence. Community Care. http://www.communitycare.co.uk/2017/02/01/experience-living-child-parent-violence/

- Coates A and Bonnick H (2016) Episode 3 - An interview with Helen Bonnick about CPV. Available at: http://adoptionandfostering.podbean.com/ 7th November 2016

- Cohen L. Manion L and Morrison K (2005) *Research Methods in Education* (6th edition) London, Routledge, Falmer

- Collins, D, (2015) Living with your child's violence. Therapy Today, Oct 2015, Vol. 26, Issue 8. P.22-26 17487846,

- Condry R and Miles C (2014) Adolescent to parent violence: Framing and mapping a hidden problem. Criminology & Criminal Justice. 2014, Vol. 14(3) 257–275

- Condry and Miles (2015) Uncovering Adolescent to Parent Violence. Palgrave

- Contact a Family (2011) Forgotten Families The impact of isolation on families with disabled children across the UK. Contact a Family. http://www.cafamily.org.uk/media/381636/forgotten_isolation_report.pdf

- Contreras L and Cano M C (2016) Social Competence and Child-to-Parent Violence: Analyzing the Role of the Emotional Intelligence, Social Attitudes, and Personal Values. DEVIANT BEHAVIOR. 2016, VOL. 37, NO. 2, 115–125

- Coogan D (2011) Child-to-Parent-Violence: challenging perspectives on family violence. Child Care in Practice Vol. 17, No. 4, October 2011, pp. 347_358

- Coogan D (2018) Child to Parent Violence and Abuse: Family Interventions with Non Violent Resistance. Jessica Kingsley Publishers

- Coogan D (2014) Responding to Child-to-Parent Violence: Innovative Practices in Child and Adolescent Mental Health. Health & Social Work Volume 39, Number 2 May 2014

- Coogan D and Lauster E (2015) Non Violent Resistance Programme Handbook for Practitioners – Responding to Child to Parent Violence in Practice, National University of Galway, Ireland, 2015 free to download from http://www.rcpv.eu/46-nvr-handbook-for-practitioners/file)

- Cottrell, B (2001) Parent Abuse: the abuse of parents by their teenage children. National Clearinghouse of Family Violence - Public Heath Agency of Canada available from http://wwwcanadiancrc.com/parent_abuse.htm

- Cottrell, B and Monk, P (2004) Adolescent to Parent Abuse: A Qualitative Overview of Common Themes. *Journal of Family Issues.* Vol. 25, No. 8: 1072-1095.

- Crotty M (1998) The Foundations of Social Research: Meaning and Perspectives in the Research Process London, Thousand Oaks, Sage

- Department of Health (2011) No health without mental health: A cross-Government mental health outcomes strategy for people of all ages. *Supporting document* – The economic case for improving efficiency and quality in mental health. Department of Health

- Dixon Jo, Lee J, Ellison S and Hicks L (2015) Supporting Adolescents on the Edge of Care. *The role of short term stays in residential care.* An Evidence Scope. NSPCC and Acton for Children

- Disability Planet (n.d) Media Representation of Disabled People access via: http://www.disabilityplanet.co.uk/parents-perspective.html

- Dugan E (2015) Kinship carers: Overwhelming public backing for improved rights and support for those who take full-time custody of their grandchildren or siblings. The Independent. Saturday 14th March 2015.

- Family Lives (2011) When Family Life Hurts: Family Experience of Aggression in Children: An update to Family Lives' October 2010 report. Family Lives.

- Family Rights Group cited in Saunders H and Selwyn J (2008) Evaluation of an informal kinship care team, Adoption and Fostering, Summer Vol 32: 2 pp 31-42 ),

- Farmer, E., Sturgess, W., O'Neill, T. and Wijedasa, D. (2011) Achieving Successful Returns from Care: What Makes Reunification Work? London: British Association for Adoption and Fostering

- Flowers R B (2000) Domestic Crimes, Family Violence and Child Abuse: A Study of Contemporary American Society. MacFarlend

- Gadamer H-G (1979) *Truth and Method* London, Shead and Ward

- Gallagher,E.(2008). *Children's Violence to Parents: A Critical Literature Review.* Master thesis. Monash University. Available online at: http://www.eddiegallagher.com.au/Child%20Parent%20Violence%20Masters%20Thesis%20Gallagher%202008.pdf

- Gordon C and Wallace K (2015) Caring for those who care for VIOLENT AND AGGRESSIVE CHILDREN. ; ADAPT (Scotland) 4th August 2015. Adapt Scotland

- Hanson, E. and Holmes, D. (2014) That Difficult Age: Developing a more effective response to risks in adolescence. Totnes: Research in Practice

- Harbin, H. T., and Madden, D. J. (1979). 'Battered parents: a new syndrome'. *American Journal of Psychiatry*, 136, 1288-1291.

- Hartley S L, Barker E T, Seltzer M M, Floyd F, Greenberg J, Orsmond G and Bolt D (2010) The Relative risk and timing of divorce in families of children with an autistic spectrum disorder. Journal of Family Psychology 2010, August 24 (4) pp449-457

- Hollins L (2017) The Reality of Physical Restraint: An Online Survey for Adoptive Parents. "A Cry for Help". Available at: https://www.researchgate.net/publication/315684427_The_Reality_of_Physical_Restraint_An_Online_Survey_for_Adoptive_Parents_A_Cry_for_Help

- Hill J and Maughan B.(eds.).(2001). *Conduct Disorders in Childhood and Adolescence*. Cambridge, UK: Cambridge University Press

- Holt A (2011) Responding to the problem of 'parent abuse'. The Psychologist. vol 24 no 3 march 2011. www.thepyschologist.co.uk

- Holt, A (2013) Adolescent-to-Parent Abuse: Current Understandings in Research, Policy and Practice. Policy Press: Bristol

- Holt A (2016) Adolescent-to-Parent Abuse as a Form of "Domestic Violence": A Conceptual Review. TRAUMA, VIOLENCE, & ABUSE. 2016, Vol. 17(5) 490-499

- Holt A and Retford S (2013) Practitioner accounts of responding to parent abuse – a case study in *ad hoc* delivery, perverse outcomes and a policy silence. Child and Family Social Work 2013, 18, pp 365–374

- Home Office (2013). 'Domestic violence and Abuse', Available at: https://www.gov.uk/domestic-violence-andabuse

- Home Office (2015) Information guide: adolescent to parent violence and abuse (APVA), Her Majesties Stationary Office (HMSO)

- Hoskins D H (2014) Consequences of Parenting on Adolescent Outcomes. Societies 2014, 4, 506–531

- Hoya-Bilbao J D, Gámez-Guadix M and Calvete E  (2018) Corporal punishment by parents and child-to-parent aggression in Spanish adolescents. anales de psicología, 2018, vol. 34, nº 1 (January), 108-116

- Ibabe, I., and Jaureguizar, J. (2012). Perfil psicológico de los menores denunciados por violencia filio parental [The psychological profile of young offenders with charges of child-to-parent violence]. *Revista Española de Investigación Criminológica, 6*, 1-19

- Ibabe, I., Jaureguizar, J. and Bentler B (2013). Risk Factors for Child-to-Parent Violence. Journal of Family Violence (2013) 28:523–534

- Ibabe,I.(2014a).Direct and indirect effects of family violence on child-to-parent violence. *Estud. Psicol.* 35,137–167.

- Ibabe I, Arnoso A and Elgorriaga E (2014b) The Clinical Profile Of Adolescent Offenders Of Child-To-Parent Violence. Social and Behavioral Sciences 131 ( 2014 ) 377 – 381

- Ibabe I, Arnoso A and Elgorriaga E (2014c) Behavioral problems and depressive symptomatology as predictors of child-to parent Violence. The European Journal of Psychology Applied to Legal Context 6 (2014) 53-61

- Jakob P (2018) Multi-stressed families, child violence and the larger system: an adaptation of the nonviolent model. Journal of Family Therapy (2018) 40: 25–44

- Kanne and Mazurek (2010) Aggression in Children and Adolescents with ASD: Prevalence and Risk Factors Journal of  Autism Developmental Disorders (2011) 41:926–937

- Kennair,N.,and Mellor,D.(2007).Parent abuse: a review. *Child Psychiatry and Human Development.* 38,203–219.

- Kennedy T. D., Edmonds W. A., Dann K. T. J., Burnett K. F. (2010). The clinical and adaptive features of young offenders of child–parent violence. Journal of Family Violence 25, 509–520

- Kershaw M, Senior Clinical Psychologist (2017) Trauma and Attachment: An Interview with Dr Marie Kershw. The Adoption and fostering Podcast, Episode 10. Available at: http://www.alcoates.co.uk/p/podcast.html

- Kuay H  S, Tiffin P A, Boothroyd L G, Tow G J, Centifanti L C M (2017) A New Trait-Based Model of Child-to-Parent Aggression. Adolescent Research Review. pp.1-13

- Lacoboni, Molnar-Szakas, Gallese, Buccino, Mazziotta, Rizzolatti (2005) *Grasping the Intentions of Others With One's Own Mirror Neuron Systems.* Available at http//www.plosbiology.org/article/info

-  Lamanna M A, Riedmann A and Stewart S D (2016) Marriages, Families, and Relationships: Making Choices in a Diverse Society. Cengage Learning, 2016
- Department for Children, Schools and Families (2009) Lamb Inquiry: Special Educational Needs and Parental Confidence. Department for Children Schools and Families

- McCrory E (Professor) The PTSD brains of Children and Soldiers, University College London reported by the BBC 18th Feb. 2016 available at: http://www.bbc.co.uk/news/health-35595086

- McElhone, G. (2017) Child to parent violence: An analysis of the perceptions of perpetrator and victim gender when considering offending and victimisation. Journal of Applied Psychology and Social Science, 3 (1), 52-73

- Maclean K (2016) Reflections on the non-accidental death of a foster carer. Adoption & Fostering. 2016, Vol. 40(4) 325–339

- McCrory Eamon (Professor) (2016) The PTSD brains of children and soldiers. University College London reported by the BBC 18th Feb. 2016 available at: http://www.bbc.co.uk/news/health-35595086

- Margolin G, Baucom B R (2014) Adolescents' aggression to parents: Longitudinal links with parents' physical aggression. Journal of Adolescent Health, 55 (2014), pp. 645-651,

- Martínez, M. L., Estévez, E., Jiménez, T. I., & Velilla, C. (2015).Child-parent violence: main characteristics, risk factors and keys to intervention. *Papeles Del Psicólogo, 36*(3), 216–224.

- Mental Health Foundation (2015) Fundamental Facts about Mental Health. Mental Health Foundation available at: https://www.mentalhealth.org.uk/sites/default/files/fundamental-facts-15.pdf

- Moorhead J (2013) The biggest problem for parents of a child with special needs? Other people. The Guardian. (16th August 2013) http://www.theguardian.com/lifeandstyle/2013/aug/16/children-disabilities-special-needs-mumsnet-campaign

- Dennis M L, Neece C L and Fenning R M. (2017) Investigating the Influence of Parenting Stress on Child Behavior Problems in Children with Developmental Delay: The Role of Parent-Child Relational Factors. Advanced Neurodevelopment Disorders (2018) 2:129–141- Published online: 6 January 2018 # Springer International Publishing AG, part of Springer Nature 2017

- Ministry of Justice (2007) Child Safety Order Guidance. Her Majesties Government: Archived 2010: http://webarchive.nationalarchives.gov.uk/20100406111257/http://www.homeoffice.gov.uk/documents/child-safety-order-guidance.html

- Moran H (revised 2015) The Coventry Grid 2 available from http://drawingtheidealself.co.uk/

- Mumdrah (2017) Collateral damage Posted on February 16, 2017 accessible at: http://mumdrah.co.uk/collateraldamage/

- National Disability Authority (2014) Chapter Five - The views and experiences of parents of children with disabilities. National Disability Authority available at: http://nda.ie/Publications/Social-Community/Independent-and-Community-Living-Focus-Group-Consultation-Report/Chapter-Five-The-views-and-experiences-of-parents-of-children-with-disabilities/

- National Scientific Council on the Developing Child. (2005/2014). *Excessive Stress Disrupts the Architecture of the Developing Brain: Working Paper 3*. Updated Edition. http://www.developingchild.harvard.edu

- Naylor C, Das P, Ross S, Honeyman M, Thompson J and Gilburt H (2016) Bringing together physical and mental health: A new frontier for integrated care. The Kings Fund. Available at: https://www.kingsfund.org.uk/sites/files/kf/field/field_publication_file/Bringing-together-Kings-Fund-March2016_1.pdf

- Nowakowski-Sims E and Rowe A (2017) The relationship between childhood adversity, attachment, and internalizing behaviors in a diversion program for child-to-mother violence. Child Abuse and Neglect 72 (2017) 266–275

- Office of Communication (OfCom) (2017) Children and Parents Media Use and Attitudes Report. Research Report published 29th November 2017, Office of Communications. UK

- Office for National Statistics (ONS) (2016) Statistics Looked After Children Office for National Statistics- https://www.gov.uk/government/statistics/children-looked-after-in-england-including-adoption-2015-to-2016 a range of statistics year on year for comparative purposes can be found at: https://www.gov.uk/government/collections/statistics-looked-after-children

- Office for National Statistics (2017) Families and Households 2017, Office for National Statistics. Released November 2017

- Pagani L, Tremblay R E, Nagin d, Zoccolillo M, Vitaro F, McDuff P (2004) Risk factor models for adolescent verbal and physical aggression toward mothers. International Journal of Behavioral Development, 28(2004), pp. 528-537,

- Parentline Plus (2008) *Aggressive Behaviour in Children: Parents' Experiences and Needs*. Parentline Plus.

- Parentline Plus (2010) *When Family Life Hurts: Family Experience of Aggression in Children*. Parentline Plus.

- Paterson R., Luntz H., Perlesz A., Cotton S. (2002) 'Adolescent violence towards parents: Maintaining family connections when the going gets tough', Australian and New Zealand Journal of Family Therapy, 232, pp. 90–100

- Pathological Demand Avoidance Society (revised edition 2016) Pathological Demand Avoidance Syndrome: A Reference Booklet for Health, Education and Social Care Practitioners. Available from www.pdasociety.org.uk

- Paulson, M. J., Coombs, R. H., & Landsverk, J. (1990). Youth who physically assault their parents. *Journal of Family Violence, 5*, 121-133

- Perry, B.D., Pollard, R., Blakely, T., Baker, W., & Vigilante, D. (1995) Childhood trauma, the neurobiology of adaptation and 'use-dependent' development of the brain: How "states" become "traits'". Infant Mental Health J, 16 (4): 271-291, 1995.

- Perry, B.D. & Pollard, R. (1998) Homeostasis, stress, trauma, and adaptation: a neurodevelopmental view of childhood trauma. Child and Adolescent Psychiatric Clinics of North America, 7; 1: 33-51, 1998.

- Perry B (2006) Applying principles of Neurodevelopment to clinical work with maltreated and traumatised children: The Neuro Sequential Model of Therapeutics in Boyd N (ed) (2006) Working with Traumatized Youth in Child Welfare. The Guildford Press. New York

- Perry, B.D., (The ChildTrauma Academy). (2013) 1: The Human Brain [Video webcast]. In *Seven Slide Series*. Retrieved from https://www.youtube.com/watch?v=uOsgDkeH52o

- Perry, B.D., (The ChildTrauma Academy). (2013) 2: Sensitization and Tolerance [Video webcast]. In *Seven Slide Series*. Retrieved from https://www.youtube.com/watch?v=qv8dRfgZXV4

- Perry, B.D., (The ChildTrauma Academy). (2013) 3: Threat Response Patterns [Video webcast]. In *Seven Slide Series*. Retrieved from https://www.youtube.com/watch?v=sr-OXkk3i8E&feature=youtu.be

- Perry, B.D.,(2014) How trauma affects child brain development. KUNM, NPR Affiliate (2014) [Radio broadcast] Retrieved from http://kunm.org/post/how-trauma-affects-child-brain-development

- Porges SW. (2001). The Polyvagal Theory: Phylogenetic substrates of a social nervous system. International Journal of Psychophysiology 42:123-146.

- Porges SW. (2003). The Polyvagal Theory: Phylogenetic contributions to social behavior. Physiology and Behavior 79:503-513.

- Reichman N E; Corman H; Noonan K (2008) Impact of Child Disability on the Family. Maternal and Child Health Journal. Springer 2008;12(6):679-683. http://www.medscape.com/viewarticle/581577_2

- Robbers SCC, Bartels M, Van Oort FVA, Van Beijsterveldt CEM, Van der Ende J, Verhulst FC, Boomsma DI, Huizink AC (in press) A twin-singleton comparison of developmental trajectories of externalizing and internalizing problems in 6- to 12-year-old children. Twin Res Hum Genet [PubMed]

- Robinson L (2010) Interventions and Restorative Responses to Address Teen Violence Against Parents. REPORT FOR THE WINSTON CHURCHILL MEMORIAL TRUST

- Rogers C (2007) Disabling a family? Emotional dilemmas experienced in becoming a parent of a child with learning disabilities- British Journal of Special Education • Volume 34 • Number 3 • 2007

- Sawyer S M, Azzopardi P S, Wickremarathe D and Patton G C (2018) The Age of Adolescence. Child and Adolescent Health. The Lancet. Published 17th January 2018

- Shonkoff, J. P., & Garner, A. (2012). The lifelong effects of early childhood adversity and toxic stress. *Pediatrics, 129*(1), e232–e246.

- Siegel, J. P. (2013). Breaking the links in intergenerational violence: An emotional regulation perspective. Family Process, 52(2), 163–178.

- Selwyn J, Wijedasa D and Meakings S (2014)  Beyond the Adoption Order: challenges, interventions and adoption disruption Research report. Department for Education, April 2014

- Selwyn J and Meakings S (2016) Adolescent-to-Parent Violence in Adoptive Families. British Journal of Social Work. 2016 Jul 46(5): 1224–1240 (Published online 2015 Sep 2, doi:10.1093/bjsw/bcv072)

- Scope (2014) New research: Parents of disabled children 'frustrated' 'stressed' and 'exhausted' by battle for support

- Silver K (2018) Adolescence now lasts from 10-24. British Broadcasting Corporation (BBC) News 19th January 2018)

- Simmons M, McEwan T E, Purcell R, Ogloff J R P (2018) Sixty years of child-to-parent abuse research: What we know and where to Go. Aggressive and Violent Behavior 38 (2018)  31-52

- Stebbings R (2001) Exploratory Research in the Social Sciences. Sage

- Stevenson L (2016) Child to parent abuse: 'I begged them to take him away'. CommunityCare October 20th 2016.

- Supin, J.  The Long Shadow:  Bruce Perry on the Lingering Effects of Childhood Trauma.  The Sun *4-13, Nov., 2016*

- Tees Local Safeguarding Board (n.d) Lack of Parental Control: Child Safety Order procedure. http://www.teescpp.org.uk/lack-of-parental-control

- The National Clearinghouse on Family Violence (2003). Parent abuse: The abuse of parents by their teenage children. Canada: Canada Government.

- The United Nations Convention of the Rights of the Child (UNCRC) UNICEF (1989) identifies 54 Articles that countries agree to adhere to. The UK signed agreement in 1990 and ratified these in 1992 by building the Articles in principle into the Childrens Act and subsequent updates including the Children and Families Act (2014)

- Thorley W (2016) EHC Plans- an opportunity to think outside of the box available at: http://www.academia.edu/31094136/EHC_plans-an_opportunity_to_think_outside_of_the_box

- Thorley and Coates (2017a) Child-Parent Violence(CPV): an exploratory exercise available at: https://www.academia.edu/30962152/Child_-Parent_Violence_CPV_an_exploratory_exercise

- Thorley W and Coates A (2017b) Child - Parent Violence (CPV): Impact on parent/carers available at: http://www.academia.edu/31433287/Child_-_Parent_Violence_CPV_exploratory_exercise_Impact_on_parent_carers_when_living_with_CPV

- Thorley W and Coates A (2017c) Child - Parent Violence (CPV): Grappling with an Enigma. available at: http://www.academia.edu/32167527/Child_-Parent_Violence_CPV_Grappling_with_an_Enigma

- Ulman, A., & Straus, M. A. (2003). Violence by children against mothers in relation to violence between parents and corporal punishment by parents. *Journal of Comparative Family Studies, 34*(1), 41-60.

- Van der Kolk B (1994) *Harvard Review of Psychiatry, 1(5), Pages 253-265*

- Van der Kolk B (2014) The Body Keeps the Score: Brain, Mind, and Body in the Healing of Trauma. Penguin Publishing Group

- Walby, S, (2009) *The Cost of Domestic Violence: Up-date 2009* (Published online: UNESCO, UNITWIN and Lancaster University, UNESCO Chair in Gender Research, 2009), p. 2

- Walliman N (2015) Social Research Methods: The Essentials. Sage.

- Wilcox, P. (2012) Is parent abuse a form of domestic violence? *Social Policy and Society* 11(2):277-288.

- Wilcox P, Pooley M, Ferrando M,  Coogan D, Lauster E, Assenova A, Mortensen U and Christoffersson I (2015) Responding to Child to Parent Violence:  Executive Summary. Available at: http://www.rcpv.eu/69-rcpv-ws3report-final-1-may-2015-pdf/file and https://www.brighton.ac.uk/ssparc/research-projects/responding-to-childto-parent-violence.aspx, http://www.rcpv.eu/resources

- Wilcox P and Pooley M (2015) Responding to Child to Parent Violence and Abuse: European Perspectives. In collaboration with National Association XXI Rhodopa Mountain Initiative, Bulgaria, Brighton & Hove City Council, England, National University of Galway, Ireland, University of Valencia, Spain and Åmåls Kommun, Sweden. Available at: http://www.rcpv.eu/69-rcpv-ws3-report-final-1-may-2015-pdf/file and https://www.brighton.ac.uk/ssparc/research-projects/responding-to-child-to-parent-violence.aspx, http://www.rcpv.eu/resources

- Winterman D (2009) Abused by their own children. BBC News Magazine. British Broadcasting Corporation (2009) Published: 2009/11/23

- World Health Organisation (version: 2016) ICD-10: International Statistical Classification of Diseases and Related Health Problems (2016) (10th Revision). World Health Organisation

- Wymbs, B. T., Pelham, W. E., Jr., Molina, B. S. G., Gnagy, E. M., Wilson, T. K., & Greenhouse, J. B. (2008). Rate and predictors of divorce among parents of youths with ADHD. *Journal of Consulting and Clinical Psychology, 76*(5), 735-744.

Printed in Great Britain
by Amazon